SURVIVAL:

MYTHS, LIES, AND FALLACY

Survival: Myths, Lies, and Fallacy by Joshua Bromley

© 2024 Joshua Bromley

First Edition
ISBN: 9798300721725
Imprint: Independently Published

DISCLAIMER

The content presented in this book is intended solely for educational purposes. It is important to note that the information contained herein is not designed to diagnose, treat, cure, or prevent any medical condition or disease. Readers are advised that this book should not be viewed as a replacement for professional consultation with a qualified healthcare provider. It is recommended that you seek guidance from your physician or healthcare professional regarding any suggestions or recommendations provided in this text.

By utilizing this book, you acknowledge and accept this disclaimer. Furthermore, both the publisher and the author disclaim any responsibility for errors, inaccuracies, omissions, or other discrepancies that may be present. The publisher and author encourage readers to take full responsibility for their own safety and to be aware of their personal limits. Prior to engaging in the practices outlined in this book, ensure that your equipment is properly maintained and refrain from undertaking risks that exceed your level of experience, skill, training, and comfort.

Dedication

To the scholars, readers, and brutally honest; chief of which is my father.

Hello! I'm Survivor Girl, an anime-inspired character born from the vibrant imagination of the author. The images and similar content in this text are created using royalty-free artificial intelligence (AI) software and are exclusively owned by the author.

This isn't a matter of liability. The author dedicates his life to academic endeavors, gathering insights across a range of topics, ultimately focusing on survivalism, self-defense, and psychology as his primary passions. Anime emerged as a hobby, adding a touch of excitement to the otherwise serious studies in those fields.

The author's role in the military revolved around two primary objectives: practicing tactical and field medicine and educating others in the medical field. Throughout this journey, he uncovered various methods to effectively train a diverse group of individuals, regardless of their backgrounds or educational experiences, in subjects that could often be intricate and complex but also perceived as "boring."

Some topics can be tedious, even for enthusiasts, but contain a wealth of vital information that could potentially save lives. One of the main focuses of his education was on how to maintain attention effectively.

Here's where I step in. My images are crafted to not only pique interest in the subject but also to infuse style into the overall presentation. They act as a refreshing break, redirecting the brain's focus onto the topic, which is especially vital for intricate, dull, or overly detailed subjects.

This image, along with other visuals like graphs, charts, and graphics, aims to draw the reader into the topic. I hope you find enjoyment in this work and the other creations by the author.

Table of Contents

Myths, Lies, and Fallacies.

Growing up in rural America, it's quite common to develop a deep appreciation for nature, especially since I live in a state famously dubbed the "natural state," celebrated for its stunning landscapes. This environment naturally led me to embrace many outdoor activities that are popular in my community, like hunting, fishing, and camping. Kids my age would often venture outside in the morning and not return until nightfall. Our outdoor adventures frequently took us into the small, wooded areas nearby, where we could easily lose ourselves in play. All these experiences contributed to a rich understanding of nature, much of which was shaped by "old timey" myths and "old wives' tales."

My experience in war transformed my scholarly ADHD-driven mind into one laser-focused on survival. Initially, my emphasis was more on self-reliance than survival itself. As a Corpsman (medic) serving with a Marine unit in various conflict zones, I quickly realized the importance of being self-sufficient, as the usual protocols for seeking help often fell short. This realization sparked my interest in how an individual can maximize their effectiveness with minimal resources and no external support. It led me to embrace the age-old philosophy of adapt, improvise, and overcome. Over time, I blended strategies from Auster medicine, ancient healing practices, and primitive techniques, ultimately honing my expertise in survival.

As soon as my mind fixated on survival as one of its main interests, I dove headfirst into research, studies, manuals, and videos. Transitioning from a beginner to a more experienced level, I observed a common pattern not only in survival but also in medicine and other fields: certain pieces of information persisted, even when they had been debunked by studies and the experiences of experts.

At the start of this writing, the COVID situation was at its peak, leading many people to isolate themselves and find themselves with a lot of free time. As a medic, I didn't have as much free time as others, but I did notice that I had more than the usual amount for someone in the military. During this period, I began gathering survival information to serve as valuable resources. My goal in writing about survival was not to simply repeat what everyone else was saying; I wanted to focus on the less obvious aspects that would be beneficial for beginners in survivalism, as well as for seasoned experts. This effort culminated in this book, which aims to debunk the most common myths, misconceptions, and fallacies related to survival.

I hope you find this information helpful! I aimed to cover a wide range of survival topics, but I might have overlooked some common myths and misconceptions. The book is packed not only with insights to clarify why certain information is misleading but also includes visuals like images, charts, and diagrams to encourage you to draw your own conclusions or kickstart your own research. These visuals are designed to make the material more engaging and interesting, rather than just presenting a wall of text. As someone with ADHD, I truly appreciate the need to give our brains a breather and avoid overwhelming them with too much information. Enjoy!

Myth: A symbolic story that elucidates a cultural belief, tradition, or natural phenomenon. Myths are frequently linked to religious faith and typically occur in an indeterminate time frame distinct from everyday human life. These narratives often include divine beings or gods participating in remarkable occurrences.

Lie: A statement that is intentionally misleading, created with the purpose of deception; a deliberate falsehood or an item meant to foster a false understanding.

Fallacy: a mistaken belief, especially one based on unsound argument or a failure in reasoning which renders an argument invalid.

Fallacy vs. a lie. a fallacy is a mistake in reasoning that weakens an argument, while a lie is a statement that is intentionally dishonest. Lie s are intentionally malicious where a fallacy may or may not be deliberately malicious in its intent.

Survival: The state or fact of continuing to live or exist, typically in spite of an accident, ordeal, or difficult circumstances.

CHAPTER ONE: MINDSET

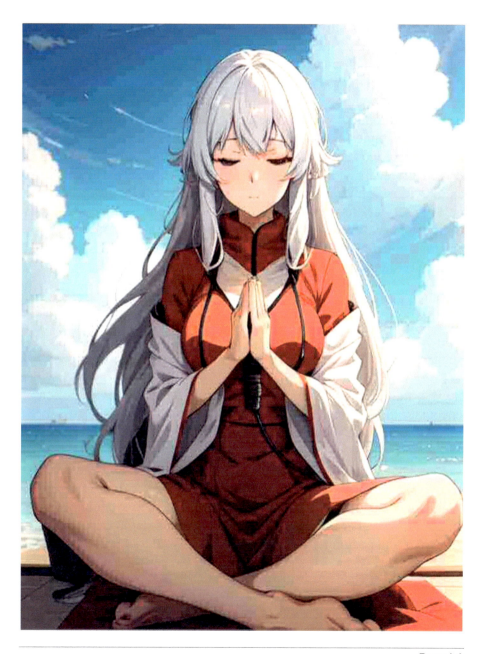

Chapter One: Mindset

Fallacy: The Seventy-Two Hour Rule.

In survival planning it is a common misconception that individuals should only anticipate being without resources for a minimum of seventy-two hours or three days. The main flaw with this belief is its limited scope.

The prevailing notion is that most utilities and resources can be back up and running within three days post-disaster. While this may be accurate for minor disasters with minimal service interruptions, it does not hold true for major disasters. On average, a major disaster can leave individuals without resources for up to two weeks. The further an individual is away from the source of the utilities the further the delay in services return to normal. This dela become more prevalent as utility service moved from local agencies to regional resources ensuring workers can take from one to six hours of travel to report to an service interruption site.

It has been demonstrated by past disasters that a supply chain may experience delays of up to fourteen days after a power loss of over forty-eight hours. Due to these and other factors, the new suggested preparation period is two weeks.

Individuals who are passionate about outdoor activities often encounter the misconception related to the seventy-two-hour rule in relation to search and rescue operations.

The initial twenty-four hours are crucial for search and rescue teams to locate casualties. Studies have shown that 85% of missing individuals are located within twelve hours, and 97% are found within twenty-four hours. This is largely due to the swift deployment of resources and personnel during the first twenty-four hours.

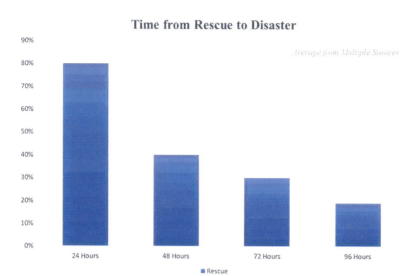

Time from Rescue to Disaster

Average from Multiple Sources

24 Hours	48 Hours	72 Hours	96 Hours

■ Rescue

In the context of search and rescue it appears that seventy-two hours is a suitable timeframe, but it is possible for an individual to be lost for a longer period. Several state agencies will search for three to ten days, and in some cases, as long as seven to fourteen days, depending on their resources and policies. The longer the search continues, the more costly it becomes for the agencies, and the chances of recovery decrease. Individuals should be prepared for the possibility of being lost for a much longer period than just three days.

YEAR	Total SAR Operations	Illness or Injured	Non-illness or Injured	Saves	Fatalities	Total Coast
2007	3593	1218	2566	1023	136	$47,354.24
2006	3623	1445	2900	1211	119	$45,248.75
2005	2430	1129	2016	402	152	$49,967.05
2004	3216	1087	3077	815	127	$35,922.18
2003	3108	1199	2162	427	124	$34,682.55
2002	4537	1338	3492	1832	129	$30,400.20
2001	3619	1502	2782	155	123	$36,830.86
2000	4869	1471	3495	709	244	$27,999.67

Search & Rescue (SAR) costs, incidents, fatalities, illness or injured, non-illness or injured, and saves associated with National Park Service SAR operations 2000 – 2007.

Common Sources of Delay:

❖ **Realize you need Help:** It is crucial at some point for an individual to acknowledge your absence or need for help and to sound the alarm.

❖ **Alarm Sounded:** When an alarm is triggered, it is essential to notify the relevant agency and ensure they are prepared to take action. For instance, in the case of a maritime incident, the Coast Guard should be alerted, whereas an emergency occurring on land would typically require the involvement of the local Sheriff's office.

❖ **Spin Them Up:** The agency needs time to coordinate, inform, and get ready. For a well-established Search and Rescue (SAR) unit, this preparation may take several hours; however, for volunteer units, it can vary from four to twelve hours.

❖ **Doing the Job:** Upon arrival at the site, finding the individual may take considerable time. This duration can vary from several minutes to a longer timeframe, depending on factors such as the landscape, the person's mobility, the time of day, and the current weather conditions.

❖ **Traffic:** Emergency responders and rescue teams reliant on ground transportation may encounter delays due to traffic congestion. Despite the use of emergency lights and sirens, many drivers do not react appropriately, resulting in further delays. Additionally, damaged and blocked roadways exacerbate these issues.

❖ **Time to Travel:** The rescue team and their gear need adequate time to arrive at the specified search locations. Various factors affect travel times, such as the terrain, fuel accessibility, weather conditions, and the kind of vehicle employed.

Fallacy: The Rules of Three.

Adhering to the seventy-two-hour guidelines also involves following the rules of three. These rules are broad concepts suggesting that an individual may succumb to an injury, illness, or disaster within a set timeframe.

It is commonly believed that an average person can survive without air for three minutes, without water for three days, and without food for three weeks. The concept that a person can only last three days without water seems to be the basis for seventy-two-hour kits. There is a common misconception among many people that they only need to prepare for three days' worth of food and water.

Everyone is unique, and various physiological differences in their bodies will ultimately dictate the actual duration of their survival. The now industry standard is to prepare for two weeks without resources. Survivalist and other individuals on the move will not be able to carry two-weeks of supplies but they can keep the two weeks' timeframe in mind when preparing supplies and equipment.

Factors determining survival timeframe

Gender

Body Type / Weight

Height

Age

Fitness / General Health

Conditioning / Activity level

Underlining Health Conditions.

Fallacy: I have seen it or read it:

There are numerous individuals who believe that possessing knowledge alone is sufficient for being prepared, whether due to ego or ignorance. Survival skills and concepts may seem straightforward when observed on television shows like those featuring Les Stroud or Bear Grylls, or when read in books, but they can actually be quite intricate. My first attempt at using flint and steel was surprisingly frustrating and took much longer than anticipated (3 hours).

It is important to remember that an individual's physical and mental state in a survival scenario will be vastly different from their comfort on a couch. Various factors, such as injury, environment, and available resources, can significantly complicate the situation.

Myth: Practicing survival is the same as survival.

There are numerous challenges that individuals face in survival situations, making tasks difficult to complete. Achieving results in a controlled environment is vastly different from achieving them when it truly matters. Scientists have found that the outcomes in controlled settings differ greatly from those in real-life scenarios, much to their disappointment. The key difference between a scientist and a survivalist learning this lesson the hard way is the risk of potential death.

To address this, individuals must consistently practice and hone their skills, as they diminish over time. Eventually, they should train in environments that closely resemble reality to improve their abilities.

Fallacy: Going at it alone.

Embarking on a solo survival journey might be a feasible short-term solution, but it is not a practical approach in the grand scheme of things. The notion of being a lone wolf is swiftly debunked in various scenarios, with injuries being a major factor. If a lone individual sustains an injury, especially one that impairs their ability to use their hands or walk, their survival prospects diminish significantly. Moreover, solitary individuals are easy targets for opportunists, particularly opportunistic groups. Conversely, joining a group boosts long-term survival as other individuals bring unique skills that can assist in survival or protection.

Myth: People will turn lawless.

The accuracy of this one varies greatly depending on the situation. For example, during Hurricane Katrina, New Orleans was devastated, and emergency services were scarce. However, reports later revealed that crime was not as prevalent as expected, with many instances of people coming together to help each other. Interestingly, most of the crimes that did occur were committed by opportunists targeting individuals in shelters rather than in the city itself. Similar patterns have been observed in other types of disasters, where groups tend to maintain some level of order even without law enforcement intervention.

Fallacy: Just leave the city.

Numerous survival guides promote the notion that people will simply flee urban areas to live off the land in nature. The crisis in Mogadishu, Somalia demonstrated that even with fertile land surrounding the city, most residents chose to remain in the deteriorating urban center as provisions ran low. Evidently, many individuals tend to adopt a passive "wait and see" approach.

The decision to leave the city or stay is heavily influenced by the surrounding environment. In numerous urban settings, departing the city may not make a difference, as one would need to travel long distances across challenging terrain before reaching a suitable environment for survival.

During my time in San Diego, I found that a large portion of the nearby areas could only be accessed via a single road. In the event that the main highway was inaccessible or heavily congested, the only means of leaving the city would involve traversing harsh terrain on foot.

Myth: Preppers/Survivalist are crazy conspiracy theorist.

Many individuals who identify as preppers or survivalists, as well as those who are drawn to prepping and survival concepts, are frequently stigmatized as being eccentric or conspiracy theorists due to the influence of television programs like Doomsday Preppers and certain political figures.

The statement is largely inaccurate. While there are a few people with extreme beliefs, particularly regarding the end of the world or societal collapse, the reality is that most individuals who engage in prepping or survivalism have experienced hardship in the past and are determined not to make the same mistakes again. Many of these individuals possess foresight and a rational belief in the potential scenarios they are preparing for. Those living in regions prone to natural disasters have been preparing for inevitable outcomes long before prepping or survivalism became popular terms.

Why People Prep

Want to be prepared.

Do more with less.

The system is fragile.

Gain self awareness.

In position to help others.

Disaster happen suddenly.

Communing with Nature

It can be fun.

Become self sufficient

Community Involvement.

The general perception of prepping and survivalism cannot be accurately determined from reality TV shows, as these shows are known to be scripted and not reflective of real-life situations. Many survival shows have been found to prioritize entertainment value over authenticity, leading to a distorted portrayal of these concepts.

It is important to consider political factors with caution when analyzing the mindset of preppers or survivalists, as politicians are often influenced by external forces rather than possessing genuine expertise on the subject. They may also have hidden agendas. Politicians frequently associate survival and prepping skills with negative connotations such as cults, terrorism, and extremism, but these skills are also utilized by military personnel, hunters, outdoor enthusiasts, first responders, and other law-abiding individuals. The key lies not in the skills themselves, but in how they are applied.

Common Risk Preparing For

Everyday Emergencies.

Natural Disasters

Man-Made Disasters

Financial Difficulties.

Challenge oneself.

Social Unrest.

Heath Hazards

Fallacy: I'll only be gone a minute

It is a widespread belief among people worldwide that they will only be away for a short while or traveling a short distance, assuming that nothing will go wrong. Surprisingly, most car accidents happen within a mile of one's home, and many individuals have experienced injury or even death during what they thought would be a quick trip. Even those who are familiar with a route or activity can find themselves in dangerous situations. For instance, Aron Ralston, known from the movie "127 Hours," went on what he thought was a routine hike, only to have his arm trapped under a boulder for five days. He had to amputate his own arm to free himself. This serves as a reminder that "complacency kills." It is crucial for individuals to consider potential risks and consequences before engaging in activities outside the norm, especially those with higher risks. Always share your plans with a trusted person when embarking on new or risky endeavors, in case of emergencies.

CHAPTER TWO: FIRE

Chapter Two: Fire

Fallacy: Rub two sticks together:

The phrase "rubbing two sticks together" oversimplifies the process of creating fire through friction. Those who think it's easy have likely never actually tried it. Watching Tom Hanks in Castaway can give you a sense of the challenges involved. While the idea isn't entirely wrong, there's more to creating fire this way than just rubbing sticks.

Factors like the materials used and the specific method employed must be carefully considered. Understanding the principles behind the technique is crucial for achieving the desired outcome; otherwise, time, energy, and resources may be wasted without any success.

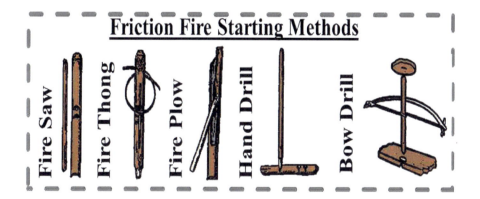

Friction Fire Starting Methods: Fire Saw, Fire Thong, Fire Plow, Hand Drill, Bow Drill

Fallacy: Eight-pointed drill

The use of an eight-sided (octagonal) drill head on the dowel for a bow friction drill has gained popularity in certain circles. It is believed that the edges of the drill head would provide better grip on the bow string, increasing friction. However, in reality, the edges end up damaging the cordage and causing the device to vibrate excessively, making the drilling process more challenging.

Fallacy: Wet matches work when dried:

Using matches that are not specifically designed for survival purposes may lead to malfunction if they get wet. Various experiments conducted by me and other survivalists have yielded inconsistent results when attempting to light a match that has been submerged in water. Due to the unpredictable nature of these outcomes, I would not rely on this method to save my life.

If the matches get wet, it is reasonable to assume that the water has affected the chemical composition of the matches, making them unable to ignite. However, this does not render them entirely ineffective. The dry matchsticks can still serve as a simple fire starter, and the match powder can be crushed and combined with fire starter to function as a fire accelerant.

Fallacy: All I need is a lighter or matches.

Lighters and matches have a similar failure rate. Lighter fuel tends to run out faster than expected. Smokers can extend the life of a lighter by using quick bursts to light up cigarettes, which can create a false sense of how long the lighter will last. Smoking materials ignite easily, requiring minimal use of the lighter. However, when using a lighter to start a fire, the flame is held longer, consuming more fuel. Additionally, the fuel in lighters can evaporate rapidly. While cheap plastic lighters may last up to a month before evaporation, Zippo™ style lighters typically last around 2 weeks. Both types of lighters can provide roughly one hour of continuous flame if fully filled.

If the fuel runs out, a lighter remains valuable as the striker can still be utilized to generate a spark. Those who are inexperienced in igniting a fire with only a spark may struggle to start a fire.

It is advisable to have various fire-starting methods on hand in case one fails. While a lighter can serve as two methods, proper training is necessary to use it effectively. Therefore, it is common for people to also carry matches and a fire steel.

Fallacy: I must start a fire right away:

Fire is a crucial aspect of survival and is often one of the initial skills a person learns. Despite its emphasis in survival media, the necessity of fire varies depending on the situation and environment. Protection from exposure should take precedence, as environmental elements can pose a greater threat than lack of food or water. In certain scenarios, proper insulation and shelter can sustain a person for days without the need for fire. A survivalist must carefully consider all priorities before investing time and resources into building a fire, as the inconvenience of relocating after the effort can be frustrating.

It's important not to be fooled by survival shows. The participants are often given staged scenarios and have had extensive practice, with some having years of experience. This can create the illusion that a fire can be started quickly. In reality, it can take the average person two to five minutes with matches or a lighter to start a fire, while other primitive methods can take an expert up to ten minutes. When determining survival priorities, individuals should consider their own level of experience.

Lie: Large fire is better than shelter.

The fire size needed depends on the environment. Cold environments may need a larger fire to produce more heat to combat the cold, while desert environments may not need a fire at all. The amount of heat needed for survival is much less than the amount needed for comfort. There are situations where a large fire is essential, such as for signaling for rescue, but in most cases, a large fire is not needed. For instance, a small teacup candle can surprisingly warm a shelter with its small flame.

It is important to prioritize the insulation of both the individual and the shelter. Additionally, the availability of resources must be taken into account. In certain environments, there may be limited materials, necessitating the conservation of firewood to ensure a sustainable supply.

Lie: Do not need fire in the desert or warm climate.

There is a common misconception that deserts are all like the ones portrayed in movies, with scorching hot temperatures and endless rolling sand dunes. However, deserts come in many different types. Deserts are actually defined by their lack of precipitation, rather than their temperature. The belief that deserts are always hot is a major misconception. Many desert environments experience winter weather at certain times of the year. Additionally, people often overlook the fact that desert temperatures can drop significantly at night compared to during the day. This rapid decrease in temperature, combined with the body's inability to adjust quickly enough, can lead to hypothermia, necessitating the need for fire in some cases. This is particularly true for individuals who find themselves lost in a desert environment without proper clothing, such as those who are running or hiking in the Mojave Desert in the southwestern United States.

Fallacy: Cannot find dry wood if it is raining.

The success of finding suitable wood for starting a fire relies on the surroundings, the skills of the individuals, and the tools at hand. Even in damp conditions, valuable resources can be discovered with the appropriate knowledge. Dry fuel may be hidden beneath layers of leaves, twigs, or at the roots of trees and shrubs. Additionally, by removing wet bark, one can access the dry wood beneath it. Dead logs can be split open to reveal inner material that is not only dry but also serves as excellent kindling.

Fallacy: Keep the fire going.

In this book, just like with other fire-related topics, the environment is crucial in determining whether the fire will continue burning or die out. The two main factors influencing this outcome are the individual's training and skill level. Many survival experts assume that beginners will struggle to start a fire, so they advise keeping it going once it's lit. Starting a fire can be challenging, especially in survival situations, so it's best to avoid having to try multiple times. Maintaining a fire is generally easier than starting one. Additionally, the availability of materials also impacts an individual's ability to sustain a fire. If resources are scarce, the person may need to put out the fire when it's not needed for cooking or warmth. Beginners should aim to keep the fire burning if there are enough resources at hand.

Survival often involves the concept of using fire to deter predators, but its effectiveness depends on the location and the types of predators present. While some predators are scared off by fire, others are attracted to it because they associate it with humans leaving food behind. On the other hand, some predators are deterred by the mere presence of humans, regardless of fire. Contrary to Hollywood portrayals, not all animals fear fire, and some may even approach it for warmth. It is important for individuals to study the behaviors of common animals in the local area to make informed decisions.

Deterred by Fire	Not Deterred
Rats	Bears
Squirrels	Racoons
Skunks	Snakes
Coyotes *	Lizards
Wolves *	
Feral Dogs *	
Extreme hunger, pack association or illness may not deter the animals	

Fallacy: Fire with Steel wool & battery or other adaptive methods.

Survival resources often showcase inventive ways to start a fire using everyday items, but many of these methods require specialized equipment or supplies used in specific ways. Chemical methods, like using potassium permanganate and antifreeze, demand a knowledge of chemistry and can pose hazards if not handled properly. Additionally, some of these supplies may be difficult to obtain or not commonly found in certain regions. For example, potassium permanganate is mostly found in European med kits and may not be effective if the kit is old. Similar chemical methods present similar challenges with obtaining the necessary materials.

Non-chemical methods also face challenges with supplies, such as the steel wool technique. Steel wool, typically used for cleaning, is now considered a less common item. Unless intentionally sought after, individuals may struggle to locate steel wool and might have an easier time finding a lighter or matches instead. Similarly, the availability of 9-volt batteries is decreasing, making them harder to come by.

Certain techniques, such as utilizing a car battery, jumper cables, and a lead pencil, are not feasible. In this approach, the lead pencil is shaved to expose the lead, and the cables are connected to each side of the pencil on the lead, causing it to heat up and create an ember. While this method may fascinate science enthusiasts, it is impractical for survival. If an individual has jumper cables and a battery, they can simply connect the cables to the battery and join the positive and negative ends to generate a spark, which can then be used to ignite the tender directly.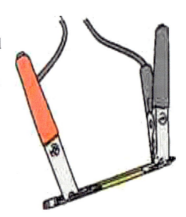

Myth: Thumb nail test for fire.

Pressing one thumb nail into a piece of wood to leave an impression is a survival technique to determine if the wood is suitable for use as friction fire material. This method is most effective with soft woods, as the ability of a material to catch fire is known as its friction point, which varies between different types of wood. Materials with low friction points, such as cottonwood, cedar, or yucca, are the best for creating friction fire. The type of friction device used will also impact the choice of material, with softer wood being more effective for the base in the fire plow method, and harder wood for the dowel. Geographic location will also determine the availability of suitable materials for fire starting methods, with some methods being better suited for certain areas. For example, bamboo is ideal for the Fire Saw but not the Fire Plow. Additionally, different materials are used in various fire devices, such as Rattan for the cord and Cedar or Balsa wood for the base in the Fire Thong.

CHAPTER THREE: WATER

Chapter Three: Water

Myth: The rule of three:

Objecting to this notion may not be well-received by survivalists, but it is important to approach it with an open mind. The belief that a person can last three days without water is highly subjective and oversimplified. The ability to survive for any length of time is influenced by various factors. One crucial factor is the individual themselves, including their weight, gender, overall health, and physical fitness level. Research on military personnel operating in challenging conditions has demonstrated that those who are physically fit can endure longer periods without food and water compared to the average person. Additionally, age is a significant factor, as the body's ability to regulate itself diminishes with age.

Similar to other topics covered in this book, this particular subject is influenced by the environment. Temperature significantly impacts the body's need for hydration, as individuals tend to feel thirstier in hotter conditions. Research indicates that altitude and sea level can also affect an individual's hydration levels.

Additionally, survival also depends on other factors. Emotional and physiological stress can lead to a faster depletion of the body's energy reserves, increasing the need for hydration. Furthermore, the level of physical activity during survival plays a role, as being sedentary requires less energy and hydration compared to being physically active. The combination of these factors ultimately determines the duration a person can survive without water.

Fluid Replacement Guide

Source: U.S. Army

Heat Category	WBGT Index (°F)	Easy Work Walking on hard surface, 2.5 mph, <30 lb. load; weapon maintenance, marksmanship training Fluid Intake (quarts/hour)	Moderate Work Patrolling, walking in send, 2.5 mph, no load; calisthenics. Fluid Intake (quarts/hour)	Hard Work Walking in sand, 2.5 mph, with load; field assaults Fluid Intake (quarts/hour)
1	78° - 81.9°	½	¾	¾ (1)*
2	82° - 84.9°	½	¾ (1)*	1 (1¼)*
3	85° - 87.9°	¾	¾ (1)*	1 (1¼)*
4	88° - 89.9°	¾	¾ (1¼)*	1 (1¼)*
5	> 90°	1	1 (1¼) *	1 (1 ½) *

* Use the amounts in parentheses for continuous work when rest breaks are not possible. Leaders should ensure several hours of rest and rehydration time after continuous work. This guidance will sustain performance and hydration for a least 4 hours of work in the specified heat category fluid needs can vary based on individual difference and exposure to full sun or full shade. Rest means minimal physical activity (sitting or standing) in the shade of possible. Body armor – add 5°F to WBGT index in humid climates. NBC (MOPP 4) – add 10°F (Moderate or Hard Work) to WBGT index. CAUTION: Hourly fluid intake should not exceed 1 ½ qts. Daily fluid intake should not exceed 12 qts.

Myth: You cannot drink too much water.

The human body constantly strives to maintain equilibrium in its functions. Proper hydration involves a delicate balance of electrolytes, water, and essential nutrients. Excessive water intake can disrupt this balance, leading to potential health issues. For instance, an overabundance of salt can prompt water to exit cells and enter the bloodstream, impairing cellular function. When the body retains too much water, it can lead to hypervolemia, also known as fluid overload or water intoxication, which may elevate blood pressure, induce swelling, and affect organ performance.

Fallacy: Drink 8 glasses of water:

It has been a common belief for many years that individuals should consume 8 glasses of water daily, with each glass being 8 ounces. The main goal is to prevent dehydration and maintain proper hydration levels. Recent research indicates that a large number of people are actually partially dehydrated or close to it, making the recommendation of drinking 8-ounces of water not entirely incorrect.

The assertion, though, is not entirely accurate due to the same rationale we explore in another part of this publication. Each person is unique with varying requirements. A person of average height, weight, age, health, and residing in a moderate temperature setting where they engage in moderate activities could suffice with just 8 ounces. However, this scenario is seldom applicable to the majority of individuals worldwide.

The environment significantly influences the amount of fluids needed to maintain proper hydration levels. Higher temperatures, especially in hot climates, require individuals to drink more fluids. Additionally, those who engage in strenuous physical activities or work will also need to consume more fluids.

Taller and heavier individuals typically require a higher water intake due to various internal factors within their bodies.

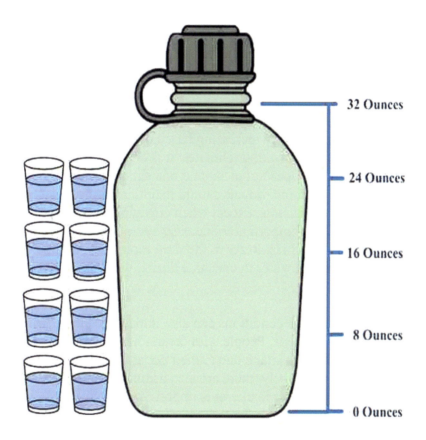

Lie: If you're not thirsty you do not need to drink:

This statement is false. The body is constantly active and functioning, which means it is constantly using up its hydration reserves. The saying goes, "if you're thirsty, you're already dehydrated."

There are limited effective ways to assess a person's hydration status. One suggested approach is to check if their urine is a light-yellow color, which indicates proper hydration. It's important to note that clear urine is a sign of overhydration, and the body takes time to process water, so a single urine check may not accurately reflect overall hydration status.

It is advisable for individuals to stay hydrated by drinking regularly, with the quantity increasing based on their level of activity and the temperature. In warmer climates, it is crucial to drink more fluids. However, this does not mean that one should drink less in cold environments. In fact, individuals should maintain their regular fluid intake in cold environments, except when engaging in increased physical activity. It is important to increase hydration when engaging in more physical activities. Refer to the fluid replacement guide for an estimate of how much water to consume during work and in different temperatures.

Different health conditions can also impact the amount of water an individual needs. People with certain health conditions may require increased water intake due to their condition or the medications they are taking. Conversely, there are also health conditions that necessitate reduced water intake. It is important for individuals with health issues to consult their doctor regarding their hydration and dietary requirements to maintain optimal health.

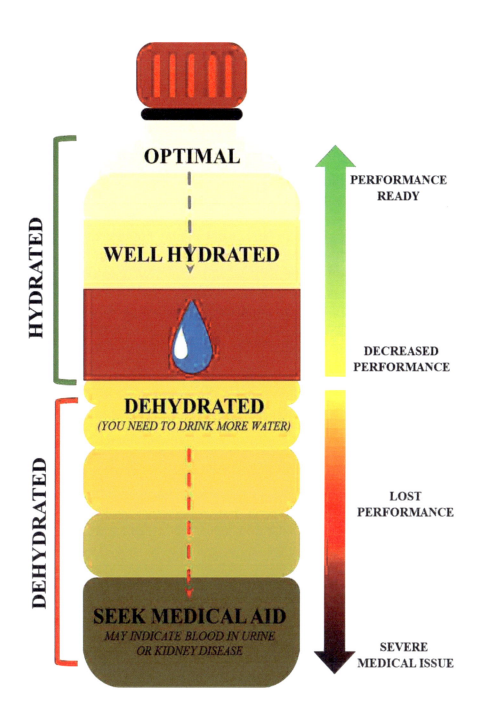

Myth: Suck on a stone for hydration:

The origins of this survival trick can be traced back to ancient times, possibly originating from observations made by primitive tribes. However, the true source remains unknown. It is important to note that this method is indeed a fallacy, as sucking on a stone will not aid in hydration whatsoever. While certain plants may be able to extract water from stones, humans are not capable of doing so. An alternative version suggests sucking on a button instead.

Sucking on a stone or similar object may not directly hydrate you, but it can stimulate saliva production, which helps lubricate a dry throat. This method is commonly used in dessert survival situations due to its ability to provide temporary relief. However, it's important to note that while the extra lubrication can alleviate dryness, it does not replace the need for water. In fact, relying solely on this method can actually accelerate dehydration since saliva production requires water.

Fallacy: Follow flying birds to find water.

Many bird species are known to frequent bodies of water, leading some to believe that following their flight path will lead to water. However, this assumption is flawed as birds in flight may not necessarily be heading towards water. They could be on migratory flight paths, meaning they may not land anytime soon or the may not be anywhere close to the observer. Following a bird could result in wasting time and energy that could have been utilized more effectively.

Lie: Running water that looks clean is safe to drink.

A recent environmental study revealed that all water sources, no matter how remote, contain some form of contamination from human pollution. Therefore, it is crucial not to assume that any water source is free from contamination, as even the tiniest microorganism can have serious health implications. This is why survivalists emphasize the importance of filtration and purification methods. It is also important to note that the appearance of water does not necessarily indicate its safety, as contaminants may not be visible to the naked eye. Surprisingly, some seemingly strange-looking water can be made safe with the right methods, while the cleanest-looking water may pose the greatest danger.

Fallacy: Boil for 10 minutes.

There are various recommendations regarding the duration for boiling water to make it safe for consumption, depending on the information source. Scientific studies indicate that boiling water at the appropriate temperature can eliminate most harmful contaminants almost instantly. Many studies suggest that simply bringing the water to a boil can make it relatively safe.

However, it is advisable to follow the US Military guideline of boiling water for 2 minutes to err on the side of caution. Boiling water for two minutes not only helps in removing contaminants but also prevents excessive evaporation. Additionally, it is important to note that boiling water does not eliminate particulates, so it is recommended to filter the water before boiling.

Fallacy: Adding salt boils faster:

It is a common belief that adding salt to water can make water boil faster, but this claim is scientifically unfounded and holds little truth.

Including this statement is important for survivalists to comprehend the scientific principle behind it. Salt actually raises the boiling point of water and reduces the amount of heat needed to increase the temperature by 1° Celsius. Consequently, saltwater boils at a lower temperature compared to pure water. Additionally, saltwater needs to reach a higher temperature before it evaporates from liquid to gas.

Simplifying in terms of survival, it is important to note that salt water requires more fuel to boil compared to freshwater. Additionally, if one is attempting to boil salt water to extract salt, the process will take a longer time due to the water needing to sit in the heat for an extended period.

When it comes to cooking, the addition of a pinch of salt can slightly increase the boiling point of water for a brief period, although the effect is minimal. Salt should be incorporated into dishes primarily for flavor enhancement or as a method to prevent certain starches from clumping together.

Fallacy: Rationing water:

In desert survival situations, rationing water may be recommended. It is crucial for individuals to monitor their body's needs and the circumstances to decide when to hydrate. Sadly, some people have been discovered deceased with full water containers. It is more likely that one will endure by consuming the water and utilizing their skills to locate additional water, rather than conserving it and waiting for more. Remember, the longer a person goes without water, the more challenging it becomes for their body to operate efficiently.

Fallacy: Eating Snow.

While technically solid water, snow does not function as expected for hydration due to its high air content. While some hydration can be obtained from consuming snow, the amount of water gained is minimal compared to the large quantities of snow that would need to be consumed. In fact, it has been reported that 10 quarts of snow would only yield one quart of water. Additionally, the low temperature of the snow can cause the body to lose heat as it melts internally, potentially leading to hypothermia. An improved approach involves melting the snow to obtain water for drinking. If starting a fire is not an option, consider placing a small amount of snow in a bottle and keeping it with you. Continuously add more snow to the bottle as it melts.

Lie: Drinking Blood.

Consuming blood does not provide hydration to the body. Despite the misconception that blood is mostly water, it is important to consider it as a source of nutrients rather than a liquid for hydration.

Some ancient cultures have a tradition of consuming blood and urine, which will be further explored later. The primary concept among these early societies was to utilize every part of the animals and avoid waste. While some primitive groups may consume animal blood for its protein and minerals, it is typically prepared or combined with other substances. Even when blood is consumed directly and in its raw form, it is often for religious purposes rather than hydration.

The body digests blood similarly to food, leading to increased energy expenditure. However, drinking blood can pose a risk of containing harmful pathogens, leading to potential health issues. In a state of starvation, the body puts strain on the kidneys, and consuming blood can exacerbate kidney damage.

Fallacy: Drink from a cactus.

While it is accurate that the fishhook barrel cactus is safe for consuming water in emergencies, it is important to note that not all cacti provide drinkable fluids. The fishhook barrel cactus is the exception, as other cacti may contain acidic or alkaloid substances that can lead to adverse effects like body aches, sharp pains, vomiting, and diarrhea. However, even the water from the fishhook barrel cactus may not be well-tolerated by everyone, potentially causing similar issues.

Prior to any claims being made, the cactus water found on retail shelves undergoes a rigorous refining process to guarantee its safety for human consumption, making it distinctly different from natural cactus water. This water is extracted from the prickly pear fruit, not the cactus root system where one would typically find water in the wild. It is important to note that excessive consumption of even commercial cactus water can lead to diarrhea.

INTERIOR OF BARREL CACTUS
-- WATERY PULP --

Fallacy: Coconut water.

Coconut water is safe to drink and good for hydration with some caveat. Technically what one is drinking from the coconut is milk and not water. Coconut milk is a diuretic meaning a person will want to urinate more often. The more a person urinates the more they dehydrate. So, an individual will still need to hydrate with water between what they drink in coconut milk to save off dehydration. The coconut also does not contain a lot of milk only have about one cup. Requiring a person to open several coconuts to get a good drink, taking a lot of effort and energy. Drinking coconut milk in large amount can also cause diarrhea in some individual along with nausea and other GI problems.

Myth: Drinking Urine.

Numerous genuine survivalists wish for the disappearance of this myth. Like blood drinking, this practice may have originated from ancient techniques of utilizing every part of the animal. Urophagia, the act of consuming urine in ancient cultures, served various purposes such as medicine, religion, or even sexual connotations, but not for hydration. Some speculate that this myth originated from military sources but all sources tracing back to pre-World War One state that urine should not be consumed.

Studies have shown that consuming urine does not actually hydrate the body, but there are no significant safety risks associated with doing so. However, since urine is a waste product, drinking it in a survival situation will only serve to further dehydrate a person. Some survivalists argue that in extreme emergencies, consuming one's own urine once may temporarily alleviate thirst, provided that the individual can overcome the gag reflex.

It is a misconception that urine is sterile. Urine may harbor bacteria that could pose a risk if ingested. While urine within the body may be free of bacteria, it can encounter bacteria at the urethral opening when expelled from the body.

Instead of using urine an improved option is to create a solar still to obtain water through evaporation. Urine can alternatively be utilized to dampen clothes or a cloth for cooling the body in dry climates.

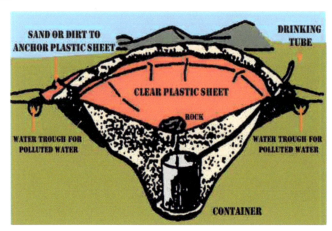

Fallacy: Fill up the Bathtub.

It is a widely accepted suggestion from various professional organizations to fill the bathtub before a disaster strikes. While many believe that the water can be used for drinking purposes during an emergency, the main purpose is to ensure there is water available for flushing toilets and washing.

It is a common misconception that the water in a tub is safe to drink simply because it comes from the same source as tap water. While this may be true initially, stagnant water in the tub can quickly become contaminated with bacteria and mold within a day. The cleanliness of the tub also plays a crucial role in the safety of the water. Unclean tubs can harbor germs that contaminate the water, while tubs cleaned with harsh chemicals can leave residues that seep into the water, posing health risks.

Customized water containers are available with a built-in tube to fill with water to prevent tub contamination and stagnation. Another option is to use clean containers like pots, coolers, and dishes before resorting to tub water. While these containers can address stagnation problems, they can also help individuals avoid contamination issues. In the absence of a commercial device, trash bags can also be used as a substitute.

Employing boiling or water purification techniques, like adding bleach, can help make water safer to drink. However, it's important to note that these methods will not address problems related to toxins or metal contamination.

Lie: Using water from the Toilet.

Water in the water heater and toilet tank comes from the same source, making it technically safe. However, issues with material and piping can cause problems. The piping used for these devices can collect bacteria and viruses that will infiltrate the water tanks. The safety of the water also depends on its original source. Gray water, a recycling method that collects water from showers, sinks, and toilets, is sometimes filtered differently from potable water and reused in toilets. This system allows for a higher percentage of impurities to remain, as the water is not intended for drinking or cooking.

It is important to note that water in the toilet bowl contains micro impurities from waste residue, even if the toilet appears clean. The belief that dogs and cats can drink from the toilet because it is safe is quite naive, as these animals have different digestive systems that can handle certain bacteria better than humans. Veterinarians often advise against allowing pets to drink from the toilet, as it is not entirely safe for them either.

Water in both the bowl and tank can pose problems with stagnant water, creating an environment for harmful bacteria like E. coli to thrive. Additionally, the water in the tank may be treated with hazardous chemicals that can accumulate and contaminate the water supply.

Lie: You can just use water from water heater.

Consuming water from the water heater raises significant safety concerns due to various factors. While the water originates from the same potable source as tap water, the water heater itself poses risks. The materials used in the heater or piping can contaminate the water, especially when heated. This process can lead to the migration of metals from the heater and pipes into the water, potentially introducing toxic substances. Additionally, plastic piping can promote germ growth, further compromising the water quality.

Caution: Bleach can be used to purify water.

The military utilizes bleach on a daily basis to treat water for consumption by using multiple methods. So, if this statement holds true, then why include it in a publication about myths, misconceptions, and falsehoods? The process is widely misinterpreted, leading to a growing misunderstanding each year, which in turn leads to a rise in accidental poisonings. Bleach is primarily intended for household cleaning. It is imperative for individuals to regard bleach as a toxic substance and handle it with the same level of caution as any other medicinal poison used to treat an ailment.

The purification of water process involves the use of pure sodium hypochlorite (NaOCL) as bleach. The labeling of products can lead to confusion, as many items are marketed as bleach but only a select few contain pure sodium hypochlorite. Bleach products marketed as laundry detergent often contain additional chemicals like dyes, cleaning agents, and perfumes, which can increase the toxicity of the bleach.

Another significant risk associated with bleach usage is the common mistake of underestimating the necessary quantity. There is a precise formula for the exact amount of water that needs to be treated. The required quantity is actually quite minimal. It is so minimal that some individuals doubt it and end up adding more, leading to unintentional poisoning. The containers used must be agitated or mixed after the bleach is added. Additionally, the water should be filtered prior to adding bleach to eliminate as many particles as possible.

Volume of Water	Amount of 6% Bleach to Add.	Amount of 8.25% Bleach to add
1 quart / liter	2 drops	2 drops
1 gallon	8 drops	6 drops
2 gallons	16 drops (1/4 tsp)	12 drops (1/8 teaspoon)
4 gallons	1/3 teaspoon	¼ teaspoon
8 gallons	2/3 teaspoon	½ teaspoon

Source: U.S. Environmental Protection Agency

Lie: Drinking water expiration.

Water does not expire, but expiration dates on water bottles are mandated for legal reasons. In 1987, New Jersey passed a law requiring all food products, including commercially sold water bottles, to have an expiration date of two years or less from the manufacture date. However, the law was later amended for bottled water.

Improper storage of water can lead to health hazards, especially when using plastic bottles. Over time, chemicals from the plastic can seep into the water, accumulating in the body and resulting in various health problems.

Improper storage can lead to bacterial growth in the water, which can pose health risks and increase the leaching of chemicals from plastic bottles. It is important to store water in a cool, dark place, away from direct sunlight and other chemical substances.

CHAPTER FOUR: FOOD

Chapter Four: Food

Lie: If an animal eats it, then it is safe.

This falsehood lacks a clear source and likely has its roots in ancient times. It is widely accepted because much of early human knowledge about nutrition comes from observing animals. Many are inclined to believe this untruth due to the close bond between humans and certain animals, such as cats and dogs, which can eat human food. However, in recent decades, veterinary science has revealed that cats and dogs have unique nutritional requirements, and the food we have been feeding them may not be suitable. Even within the animal kingdom, to which humans belong, different species have vastly different digestive systems.

These differences are not only anatomical but also extend to the types of bacteria present in the stomach and intestines, which can either aid or hinder digestion. These variations allow animals to consume substances that humans cannot, and some animals can even ingest poisonous substances without any harmful effects.

One similar expression is "what a monkey consumes is also suitable for humans." While there is some truth to this, as monkey diets closely resemble those of humans, they also consume items that are difficult for humans to digest, such as leaves, flowers, and bark. It is advisable to only consume fruits and nuts that are familiar to humans, rather than blindly following a monkey's diet. Observing a monkey's eating habits can guide a survivalist to edible food. However, it is important to exercise caution around monkeys, as many species can be highly aggressive.

Fallacy: It is safe to eat raw meat and seafood.

There exists a significant disparity between the sushi/sashimi platter served at the local restaurant and the raw fish caught in the wild. The raw fish available in markets and eateries undergo rigorous quality control measures to ensure their relative safety, yet the occurrence of 1.2 million cases of food poisoning annually indicates that issues persist. Even mild food poisoning can pose a serious threat to survival. All food, including those traditionally consumed raw, should be cooked whenever possible in a survival situation. It is imperative not to make assumptions about food. Raw meat or poultry should never be consumed, as they contain harmful bacteria that often result in dysentery, which can ultimately lead to death. Please refer to the appendices for a list of raw food guidelines.

Fallacy: Food is top priority.

One common assertion found in survival forums is that food should be given higher importance than other survival considerations. This is due to the significant amount of attention given to food in prepping discussions, which can be confusing for those new to the topic. However, as individuals delve into research on survivalism, prepping, and disaster preparedness, they will learn that three priorities take precedence over food. The first priority is to eliminate or escape from danger. The second priority varies between water procurement and exposure, depending on the environment and circumstances. Understanding the previously mentioned rules of three demonstrates the relatively low priority of food in survival, at least initially. The rule of three is an oversimplified concept that can be misleading, leading to the next section.

Fallacy: One can survive three weeks without food.

The rule of three, when applied to water, is not realistic for the same reasons it is unrealistic when related to food. A person's food requirements are influenced by factors such as environment, health, injury, and activities, just like water. While some people may survive three weeks without food, it is important to understand that the actual time frame is much shorter. Advocates of the rule of three often overlook the psychological aspect of hunger. The pain of hunger intensifies over time, causing significant psychological distress that can impair decision-making. There have been numerous documented cases of individuals taking their own lives due to hunger before actually dying from starvation.

Fallacy: You can survive on survival food alone.

When discussing survival food, the focus is often on unconventional sources such as plants or unique animals that survivalists recommend foraging in the wild, rather than relying on traditional supermarket fare. Examples include pine needle tea, dandelions, or wild berries. However, a major drawback of survival foods is that the quantity that can be gathered is usually insufficient to meet a person's nutritional needs for survival. Additionally, these unconventional foods may not always provide the specific nutrients required for optimal health. The availability of such resources is heavily dependent on the surrounding environment, with some regions being more abundant than others. Those who advocate for this approach are typically situated in temperate climates and prioritize wilderness survival, often overlooking the diverse environments found across the globe.

SURVIVAL FOOD PYRAMID

Fallacy: I can just forage for food.

Hunting was the main method of food procurement for many years before farming due to the necessity of specific knowledge required to identify and locate appropriate food, as well as the physical fitness required for gathering and carrying the food. Additionally, the limited availability of food sources in the wild meant that excess food could not be stored, requiring it to be consumed immediately. The unpredictability of nature and competition from other animals also made it challenging to rely solely on wild food sources. As a result, early tribes primarily gathered berries, roots, and seasonal fruits for sustenance.

Most of the plants available in grocery stores today have been developed through centuries of farming, making their wild counterparts unrecognizable or non-existent. For instance, the familiar orange color and triangular shape of carrots are the result of centuries of cultivation, while wild carrots are white and look like any other root. Similarly, broccoli would not exist without farming efforts. Additionally, some edible plants, like potatoes, are easily recognizable, but their actual plants may not be as familiar to the untrained eye. The following is a list of edible wild plants, although it is not exhaustive.

Common Name	Scientific Name
Amaranth	Amaranthus Retroflexus
Asparagus	Asparagus Officinalis
Burdock	Arctium Lappa
Cattail	Typha
Clovers	Trifolium
Chicory	Cichorium Intybus
Chickweed	Stellaria Media
Curled Dock	Rumex Crispus
Dandelion	Taraxacum Officinale
Fireweed	Epilobium Angustifolium
Plantain	Plantago
Prickly Pear Cactus	Opuntia
Sheep Sorrel	Rumex Acetosella
White Mustard	Synapsis Alba
Wood Sorrel	Oxalis

Fallacy: I can survive off (insert here) alone.

Consuming a single type of food does not provide the essential macronutrients needed for survival. Restricting oneself to only one type of food can lead to various health issues and diseases. This is particularly concerning for prolonged periods of time. While the body can temporarily survive on a single type of food with sufficient water intake, it may still experience minor complications.

A diet solely consisting of plant-based foods (fruits and vegetables) lacks fats and proteins. Fats are crucial for cognitive functions, energy production, metabolism, and muscle strength. A significant concern is the drastic decrease in energy levels as one continues to deprive themselves of other sources of nutrition.

Fruits and vegetables are rich in nutrients that are unique and not found in other food sources. The absence of these nutrients can result in specific health issues. Scurvy, a condition caused by a deficiency in vitamin C, was a common problem for ancient sailors. Vitamin C is mainly obtained from fruits and vegetables, while meat lacks fiber. Insufficient fiber intake can lead to constipation, a painful condition that may result in severe complications. Consuming only lean meat without fats can also lead to various diseases. For instance, exclusively eating rabbits can lead to a condition known as "rabbit starvation," as observed by early arctic explorers. This condition, now referred to as protein poisoning, is a type of malnutrition that can cause symptoms like nausea, vomiting, diarrhea, and ultimately, death.

A drawback of diets consisting solely of fish is that fish tend to retain heavy metals and other pollutants, which can ultimately lead to poisoning the human body. One such pollutant is mercury, which may be the primary source of mercury contamination in humans.

Fallacy: Hunting is the best way to get food.

Hunting is a multifaceted skill that encompasses various equally intricate skills. It involves the identification, tracking, killing, butchering, and preparation of the prey, each of which requires significant effort to master. Additionally, a hunter must be adept at understanding the type of prey found in their surroundings. Proficiency in hunting in one location does not guarantee proficiency in another. Furthermore, hunters may encounter challenges when hunting unfamiliar prey, especially if they are not accustomed to the equipment they are using. Even the most skilled hunter may struggle when relying on methods unrelated to firearms.

Trapping presents its own set of challenges, as it necessitates the expertise to set the trap, as well as the effort and resources to maintain the traps. Numerous hunters have encountered situations where they have checked their traps only to discover that the prey has escaped or that something else has taken it.

Fishing is considered the most straightforward approach, yet it is not without its challenges. Fishermen must locate a reliable fishing spot, have sufficient bait, and possess the necessary equipment to successfully catch fish.

Fallacy: Universal Edibility Test.

There is a dangerous fallacy that lacks scientific evidence to support its effectiveness. Nevertheless, it is still viewed as an acceptable last resort. Many survivalists believe that attempting this test is preferable to starving to death. The test is perilous because even slight contact with certain plants can trigger a severe allergic reaction in some people. Below is considered one of the most cautious examples of the edibility test. The Army acknowledges that despite taking all precautions, some individuals may have different reactions. Another issue with the test is that it can take up to 16 hours just to safely test one part of a plant, which many will find challenging when consumed by hunger.

U. S. Army Edibility Test

1. Test Only one part of a potential food plant at a time

2. Separate the plant into its basic components
(leaves, stems, roots, buds, and flower)

3. Smell the food for strong or acid odors.
Remember, smell alone does not indicate a plant is edible or inedible

4. DO NOT eat for 8 hours before starting the test

5. During the 8 hours you abstain from eating, test for contact poisoning by placing a piece of the plant part you are testing on the inside of your elbow or wrist. Usually 15 minutes is enough time to allow for a reaction

6. During the test period, take nothing by mouth except purified water & plant part you are testing.

7. Select a small portion of a single part & prepare it the way you plan to eat it

8. Before placing the prepared plant part in your mouth, touch a small portion (a pinch) to the outer surface of your lip to test for burning or itching.

9. If after three minutes there is no reaction on you lip, place the plant part on your tongue, holding it there for 15 minutes.

10. If there is no reaction, thoroughly chew a pinch and hold it in your mouth for 15 minutes. DO NOT swallow.

11. If no burning, itching, numbing, stinging, or other irritation occurs during the 15 minutes, swallow the food.

12. Wait 8 hours. If any ill effects occur during this period. Induce vomiting and drink a lot of water.

13. If no ill effects occur, eat 0.25 cup of the same plant part prepared the same way. Wait another 8 hours. If no ill effects occur, the plant part as prepared is safe for eating.

CAUTION: test all parts of the plant for edibility, as some plants have both edible & inedible parts. DO NOT assume that a part that proved edible when cooked is also edible when raw. Test the part raw to ensure edibility before eating raw. The same part or plant may produce varying reactions in different individuals.

Source: U.S. Army Survival Manual

Fallacy: Mushrooms are a good source of food.

This assertion would be accurate were it not for the challenge of distinguishing between edible and poisonous mushrooms. Numerous mushrooms bear a striking resemblance to one another. There are nearly 10,000 varieties of mushrooms, with only around 250 being safe for consumption. Additionally, some of these edible mushrooms require specific preparation in order to be safe to eat. Even the most experienced scientist may struggle at times to differentiate between edible mushrooms and other types. From a statistical standpoint, an individual is more likely to encounter poisonous mushrooms than safe ones. There are fourteen syndromes that can result from consuming the wrong mushrooms, ranging from hallucinations to various toxicities.

Myth: Twinkies do not expire.

The origin of this myth remains uncertain, however, there is a widespread belief that twinkies never expire due to the high number of preservatives they contain. The shelf life of twinkies is only 25 – 30 days. Hostess' research and development team conducted a study on the shelf life of twinkies, debunking this myth.

Myth: 5 second rule.

A common myth that individuals often hear during their formative years is the belief that swiftly picking up dropped food from the floor prevents bacteria and viruses from contaminating it, thus reducing the risk of falling ill.

It is widely believed that the notion of the "five-second rule" is a misconception, as bacteria, the primary cause of many foodborne illnesses, can contaminate food almost immediately upon contact. Research has consistently shown that this rule is not based on scientific evidence. Furthermore, studies have demonstrated that even with thorough cleaning, some bacteria can still be present on surfaces such as floors.

On the other hand, the notion that dry food, rather than wet food, is safer according to the 5-second rule is incorrect. While it is accurate that dry food is less prone to collecting dirt or grime, bacteria can still easily adhere to it regardless of its moisture content.

It is advisable to discard any food that has come into contact with the floor. However, in a survival situation where food is scarce, it is suggested to wash the food or boil it in water if feasible. Nevertheless, there is no guarantee that this will prevent illness.

Fallacy: Just set a trap.

Numerous survival kits prioritize the necessity of having materials to set up traps as the main method of obtaining food. Trapping can be quite challenging, even for those with expertise. The complexity of trapping was such that, at one time, it was considered a profession in its own right. Trapping requires a deep understanding of the prey being targeted and the ability to build the appropriate trap for that specific prey.

There exist two classifications of traps: restraining and killing, each designed with specific construction methods suitable for different types of animals. It is crucial to understand that traps do not differentiate between the animals they ensnare. Various species necessitate distinct trap types, like cages for birds or snares for smaller game. Survival guides frequently emphasize trapping small mammals due to the extensive coverage this topic requires in literature. Individuals must also possess the know-how to strategically place traps; otherwise, they may end up constructing traps that are ineffective in catching any prey.

Trap Types
Snares
Pits
Cages
Glue
Deadfall
Mechanical

Fishing in the same realm as trapping is not as simple as some survival experts may suggest. The development of specialized equipment for fishing is not without reason, as catching a fish with just a single fishing line and a few hooks is unlikely to yield any results.

Here is a compilation of fundamental trap categories. It is important to note that each category has variations for either restraining or killing. Furthermore, each trap type also varies based on the targeted animal, whether it is a mammal, fish, or bird, and on average, each type will have at least three variations for each animal category.

Fallacy: Berries are safe.

There are numerous examples of people surviving on wild berries. In many areas, it is a popular pastime to forage for wild berries, with great success in places where the plant is well-known, and its location is familiar. The safety of berries depends on the type of plant, and while not as complex as learning about mushrooms, some level of familiarity is necessary to ensure that the berries are not poisonous. One advantage of berries is that even the poisonous ones may not be lethal, but they can cause illness leading to dehydration, vomiting, diarrhea, and other health issues. According to multiple sources, approximately 10% of white or yellow berries are safe, 50% of red berries are safe, and 90% of blue or black berries are safe. Therefore, when trying to survive, it is advisable to locate blue or black berries, or take a chance with red ones.

Fallacy: Hunting at night is a good idea.

One suggestion for survival that has been proposed is the concept that many fish and edible animals are nocturnal, making hunting and fishing at night a feasible option for survivalists. However, hunting at night during a survival situation is not advisable for several reasons. The absence of light sources increases the risk of tripping and injuring oneself. Hunting and fishing are already challenging during the day due to limited visibility, let alone attempting to do so at night. Those who are successful at night hunting typically use specialized equipment, which is not readily available in a survival scenario with limited gear and resources. Most experts recommend resting at night to avoid the risk of injury, and trapping nocturnal prey is often suggested as a more viable option for those with the necessary knowledge and skills.

CHAPTER FIVE: SHELTER

Chapter Five: Shelter

Fallacy: Shelter means coverage.

There is a small misunderstanding regarding the construction of survival shelters, as some may wrongly assume that any shelter will suffice in a survival scenario. It is important to understand that merely building a shelter does not guarantee its effectiveness.

In certain environments, an individual requires more than just a roof to ensure survival. While many focus on constructing a shelter, they often overlook the importance of proper bedding. Sleeping directly on the ground can lead to heat loss through conduction. The absence of bedding can lead to exposure issues more quickly than a shelter without a roof.

Survivalists must also have knowledge of various types of shelters and the materials used to construct them. While some may not consider snow to be a suitable shelter material, igloos demonstrate that even unconventional materials can offer sufficient protection when properly utilized.

Fallacy: Build with plenty of room.

Numerous materials will be used to construct a shelter with ample space, however, the larger the space within the shelter, the more of an area that needs to be heated. A more compact shelter will result in less heat escaping. In comparison the principle of layering clothing involves trapping heated air between each layer, enabling the heat to circulate back to the body.

Myth: Build close to water.

There is a common misunderstanding when survivalists establish their base near water sources. Many people mistakenly believe the recommendation to build close to water means building the shelter directly next to the water or in close proximity to it. However, what they mean is build close enough to the water so that one does not have to exert too much energy in fetching water.

Survivalists, on the other hand, prefer not to build right next to the water due to various environmental factors. In certain environments, water levels can unexpectedly rise and flood an individual's campsite. Additionally, extreme weather conditions can lead to the destruction of a campsite through flooding, mudslides, and soil erosion. Animals often gather around bodies of water and can disrupt a campsite. Certain animals pose a potential threat to campers.

Fallacy: Just build an igloo or ice trench.

Building shelters using snow and ice is a highly challenging task that demands specific expertise and a variety of tools. Advocates of this practice may showcase their skills, but they typically rely on tools that are not commonly found among survivalists.

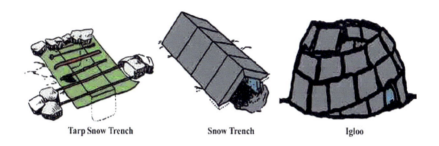

Tarp Snow Trench   Snow Trench   Igloo

Lie: All Base Layers are equal.

A base layer is the undergarment worn beneath outer clothing to provide insulation. There is a common misconception that all base layers are equally effective, perpetuated by those who have not conducted any research but rely on personal experience. Cotton has long been the go-to material for base layers, known as "sniffle gear," due to its versatility. However, one drawback of cotton is that it loses its insulating properties when wet, as it can retain moisture much longer than synthetic or wool materials.

Fallacy: Building a fire in the cave.

      It is not common to find suitable caves for shelter, despite what is often portrayed in the media. In the rare occasion that individuals do find a cave to seek shelter in, they may encounter other living beings already occupying the space. If one does decide to use a cave for shelter, caution must be exercised when building a fire. The enclosed space can trap smoke, potentially leading to suffocation or carbon monoxide poisoning. Additionally, heating rocks in a cave can cause them to expand and potentially break, resulting in injury from falling debris or even a cave-in.

CHAPTER SIX: ANIMALS

Chapter Six: Animals

Fallacy: Predators are a major threat.

The media often enjoys recounting tales of humans triumphing over dangerous beasts in various fantastical stories, but truly perilous predators are quite rare, and those that are dangerous can usually be avoided. In extremely rare cases, alpha predators, commonly referred to as "man eaters," have made appearances throughout history, but they typically target isolated individuals or the weak. Most animals, even the dangerous ones, tend to steer clear of humans. The instances where animals have attacked have often occurred because the human stumbled upon them, or because the animal was old and sick.

The hippopotamus is responsible for approximately 500 human deaths annually, making it the most dangerous animal to humans. However, it's important to note that these fatalities are typically related to individuals encroaching on the hippo's territory. On the other hand, mosquitoes are considered the deadliest animals in the world due to their ability to transmit more deadly viruses than any other creature. Additionally, bees are responsible for causing numerous anaphylactic shocks.

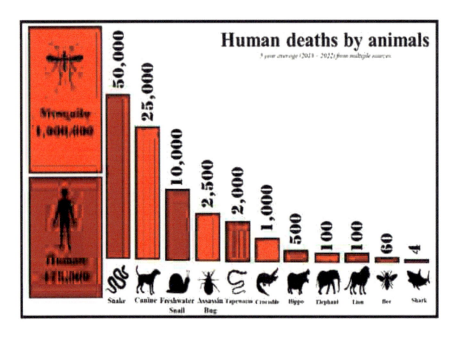

Fallacy: Predators as the only threat.

     Predators are often highlighted as a major threat in survival situations, but there are numerous other concerns to consider. In many cases, the environment poses the greatest danger, as exposure to extreme temperatures can be fatal much more quickly than an encounter with a wild animal. Dehydration is a significant risk, and there is also the potential for self-injury due to environmental hazards.

Fallacy: Something will get me first:

     Numerous individuals who spend time outdoors will argue that they are more likely to be affected by exposure and thirst than by any type of animal. In fact, a person is at a greater risk of dying from exposure and thirst than from encountering a predator. It is important to note that most animals will steer clear of humans, even if they enter their territory, unless they come across them directly.

Myth: Pee around camp site to warn off animals.

Animals use urine to mark their territory and deter other animals from entering. There is a common belief that urinating around a campsite will keep animals, especially predators, away. However, this is usually not the case. In fact, many animals, such as bears, are attracted to the smell out of curiosity or because they associate humans with food. Additionally, urine can attract bugs that carry diseases and cause other problems. It is generally advised to use the bathroom at least 200 meters away from the campsite.

	Water Source	Food Service	Berthing
Latrine	100 Feet	300 Feet	50 Feet
Cook camp			20 Feet
Food Catch			10-50 Feet
Butchering			300 Feet
Water Source			200 Feet

Myth: Hit the shark on the nose.

It is often claimed that striking a shark on the nose will deter it from attacking, but this is a misconception that is quite challenging to execute. Maneuvering in water is strenuous for humans, while sharks have the upper hand in their natural environment. Moreover, accurately hitting a target while swimming is already difficult, and the water's distortion effect further complicates the task. Therefore, landing a precise punch under these circumstances is nearly impossible.

In the event of a shark attack, the pain from the bite and the shark's erratic movements can make it challenging to accurately aim and strike. A more effective approach when being bitten by a shark is to target its eyes.

Myth: Poke the shark in the eye.

Punching a shark in the nose or poking it in the eye are both ill-advised actions for the same reasons. Most creatures, including humans, will instinctively release their prey when poked in the eye. Therefore, using this tactic to escape an attack is a viable option, as the shark is likely to let go and swim away. However, it is important to note that the shark may return for another attempt, although this is unlikely. Additionally, this method does not serve as a preventive measure, as it is challenging to execute before the shark bites and even more difficult to accomplish once the attack has begun.

Lie: You can outrun a bear.

The simple response is negative. Bears can reach speeds ranging from 25 to 35 mph, significantly surpassing the average human running speed of 9 mph. Although the fastest recorded human running speed was 27 mph, it is likely that even the slowest bear could overtake. The misconception that bears are unable to run downhill is inaccurate, as they can run at nearly full speed both uphill and downhill.

Fallacy: Climbing away from bear.

Unfortunately, running, playing dead, and attempting to climb a tree are all ineffective methods of escaping from bears. Some bear species, like Grizzlies and Black bears, are capable of climbing trees, and they are also fast enough to catch a person before they can successfully climb to safety.

Myth: Play dead when attacked by a bear.

Playing dead is generally accurate when encountering a grizzly bear, however, the same does not apply to black bears. It is debatable on whether pretending to be dead would be effective against a grizzly bear. A more effective approach would be to stand upright, extend your arm, and communicate with the bear to show that you are a human.

It is advised to assume a passive position when encountering a brown or grizzly bear, by lying on one's stomach and spreading their legs. Remaining still in this position until the bear leaves is recommended, as fighting back may lead to further aggression from the bear.

When encountering a black bear, avoid pretending to be dead and seek refuge in a safe location like a building or vehicle if available. In the event of an attack, defend yourself by utilizing any means necessary, focusing on the bear's face and snout.

Lie: Bear spray is more effective than a gun.

Firearms present a challenge as they demand a certain level of skill, which must be replicable in high-pressure scenarios involving a large, aggressive, and fast animal. The efficacy of firearms is also contingent on the type and caliber, as well as the precise placement of the round in a vital area of the bear. Striking a non-lethal spot may further enrage the bear.

Advocates of using spray instead of firearms emphasize the importance of individuals being skilled in operating the device and being knowledgeable about factors like wind that can affect its effectiveness.

Some other Bear necessities:

It is inaccurate to claim that once a bear has tasted human food, it will no longer consume wild food. Bears have specific nutritional needs and will consume whatever is readily available, with human food often being easily accessible.

An additional misconception regarding bears is that they have a fear of fire. Placing a torch near a bear's face could potentially trigger a defensive reaction and prompt the bear to run away, although this outcome is not certain.

Standing bears often stand on their hind legs to get a better view, not necessarily to attack. They may adopt this posture out of curiosity or to interact with their surroundings. It can serve as an alert, a sign of curiosity, or a precursor to an attack. Bears that exhibit aggressive behaviors such as huffing, teeth clacking, and ground slapping are attempting to intimidate and may attack if the threat persists. In some cases, a charging bear may be a bluff, with the bear stopping abruptly to growl, click its teeth, and huff as a warning for the individual to retreat.

Bear bells can be effective in certain regions where bears have become accustomed to associating the sound with humans. However, not all bears are familiar with them, and individuals may still unexpectedly encounter a bear. A more reliable alternative is to speak loudly or sing to alert the bear of your presence.

It has been determined that it is not dangerous to enter bear country while menstruating. Research has shown that bears tend to ignore used tampons left by researchers, and there is no evidence of a correlation between bear attacks and individuals who are menstruating. Most bear attacks are accidental, occurring when a bear unexpectedly encounters a human while searching for food, or when a human startles a bear, enters its territory during the wrong season, or gets too close to its cubs. To err on the side of caution, it is advisable to store all hygiene products in bearproof containers.

Fallacy: Bears sleep all winter.

Bears do not hibernate solely due to cold temperatures; rather, their sleep is a response to the scarcity of food during winter months. They possess an evolutionary adaptation that enables them to lower their body temperature and gradually metabolize stored fats and nutrients. When food is readily available, bears remain active, but as temperatures decrease and food becomes limited, they enter longer periods of sleep to conserve energy and minimize nutrient depletion. Even in the harshest winter conditions, bears can awaken to address threats such as predators encroaching on their territory or adverse weather affecting their dens. Additionally, not all bears utilize caves for shelter; some construct dens using various natural materials, including fallen leaves.

Myth: Touching a toad causes warts.

Warts are the result of viruses that lead to a skin infection. It is important to note that warts are not caused by toads, their secretions, or any other factors related to them. However, contact with toads and frogs may occasionally result in skin irritation and other health issues.

The myth is believed to stem from the stereotypical image of how ancient witches were perceived, as well as their supposed connection to toads as part of their magical lineage. However, there is no historical or scientific evidence to support this association.

Myth: Animals cannot detect earthquakes.

This legend is not well comprehended and challenging to definitively prove. While it is commonly thought to be false, there is some evidence suggesting that animals have the ability to forecast earthquakes in advance.

It is unclear whether animals possess a "sixth sense" linked to disaster detection. However, it is conceivable that animals, due to their stronger reliance on nature, are more attuned to their surroundings than humans. As a result, they may sense changes preceding a disaster faster than individuals can.

Fallacy: Animals predict the weather.

The primary issue with the belief that animals can predict the weather lies in the assumption that humans comprehend animal behavior. Despite coexisting with certain animals like dogs and cats for thousands of years, our understanding of their behavior remains limited. While there is some evidence supporting the idea that animals can predict the weather, much of it is attributed to their heightened sensitivity to the environment. Animals can detect subtle changes in their surroundings faster than humans. This does not necessarily mean that they are predicting the weather, but rather that they are perceiving it more quickly than humans. Additionally, some of the animals' senses contribute to their ability to pick up on environmental cues. For instance, cats' superior hearing allows them to hear thunder from a greater distance than humans, enabling them to prepare for rain earlier. Animals also react in various ways for both environmental and emotional reasons. For example, a dog may retreat to its kennel and hide under a blanket before it rains, but this behavior could also be driven by emotional factors. Therefore, while an individual may be preparing for rain, their dog could simply be experiencing depression. Animals' heightened sensitivity to the environment is beneficial in predicting certain weather patterns. For instance, insects tend to disappear before a storm, and if they are absent in large numbers, the day will likely be clear. Additionally, aquatic life tends to move to deeper water before a storm.

Fallacy: chameleons change color for camouflage.

A chameleon's capacity to alter its color is influenced by various factors, including temperature and the animal's emotional state. Additionally, chameleons may change color in response to social interactions, such as asserting dominance over a male, displaying submission to a rival, or signaling readiness to mate. Furthermore, the phenomenon of camouflage may stem from the inherent coloration of the chameleon, as different species tend to exhibit hues that closely resemble the colors of their native environments.

Myth: Piranhas as deadly predators.

The perceived threats posed by piranhas are largely overstated. They are not capable of consuming a human body within seconds. Piranhas are generally shy and cautious scavengers rather than aggressive hunters. However, this does not imply that they are entirely safe; they can exhibit aggressive behavior, particularly during drought conditions and mating seasons. On average, there are about 200 reported attacks annually, with experts suggesting that these incidents often result from misidentification, such as when piranhas mistakenly bite humans while foraging for food dropped by tourists or when large groups become trapped in a shrinking water source and face starvation. Many piranha species primarily feed on carrion, as well as fruits, fish scales, and occasionally nibble on the fins of other fish. While fatalities do occur from time to time, they are relatively rare.

Fallacy: Birds always fly towards water.

  Birds fly to various destinations such as breeding grounds, food sources, nests, and to other birds. They can travel great distances, so even if a bird is flying towards water, it could be several miles away. Some bird species, like ducks, geese, and flamingos, are commonly found near water. The presence of large groups of birds flying low in a particular area may suggest that water is nearby.

Fallacy: Birds fly south for the winter.

  This explanation oversimplifies the concept of migration. While some species do migrate towards warmer climates in the winter, others migrate to higher or lower elevations. Additionally, there are species that stay in the same place throughout the year. Migration in many species is driven by the search for food rather than warmth, as they move to areas with better foraging opportunities rather than just warmer locations during certain times of the year.

Myth: Zigzag if chased by an alligator.

The agility of alligators is often underestimated. Despite their short legs, which are believed to limit their mobility, they are quite nimble. While they may lack endurance and can only sprint for short distances, it is still advisable for a person to try to outrun them.

CHAPTER SEVEN: FIRST-AID

Chapter Seven: First aid

Fallacy: First Aid Kits.

Store-bought first aid kits lack the necessary components for effective emergency medical care. While these kits are marketed to instill a sense of security, they are primarily designed for minor injuries. EMTs and military medics carry extensive supplies for a reason. For true emergency situations like survival, disasters, or tactical environments, individuals should consider creating their own customized kits. While a commercial kit can be a starting point, proper training and experience are essential for enhancing and tailoring it to specific needs.

Quantity	Item	Measurement
2	Absorbent Compress Dressing	5" x 9"
25	Adhesive Bandages (band-aid)	Assorted Sizes
1	Adhesive Cloth Tape	10 yards x 1"
5	Antiseptic Wipe Package	
5	Package Aspirin	
2	Emergency Blanket	
1	Breathing Barrier (w/1-way valve)	
1	Instant Cold Compress	
2	Pair Non-latex Gloves	Large
2	Hydrocortisone Ointment Package	1 gram each
1	Gauze Role	3" wide
1	Roller Bandage	4" wide
5	Sterile gauze pad	4" x 4"
1	Oral Thermometer	
2	Triangular Bandages	
1	Tweezers	
1	First Aid Instructions	

Recommendations from the American Red Cross of Basic First Aid Kit for a family of four.

Note: Interaction with first aid kits can occur either through a kit purchased for personal use or those provided within the workplace. Workplace first aid kit requirements are determined by the Occupational Safety and Health Standards (OSHA) 1910.151, which references the American National Standards Institute (ANSI) Z308.1-2021 for kit inventory specifications, dividing them into classes A & B. Interestingly, the ANSI list is not available for free and can cost up to two hundred dollars. As a result, many companies opt to use the Red Cross inventory instead of the ANSI version. It is important to note that some companies, mandated to comply with OSHA standards, may unknowingly purchase lower quality commercial kits, mistaking them for adequate. Even experienced safety inspectors may consider having a commercial kit sufficient without recognizing the distinction.

| Class A | | Class B | | |
Quantity	Item	Quantity	Item	Measurement
1	4 x4 Gauze	1		4"x 4" (10x10 Cm)
16	Adhesive Bandage (band aid)	50		1" x 3" (25x75 cm)
1	Adhesive Tape	2		2.5 yd (23 m) total
10	Antibiotic Application	25		1/7 oz (0.5g)
10	Antiseptic	50		1/7 oz (0.5g)
1	Burn Dressing (gel soaked)	2		
10	Burn Treatment	25		1/32 (0.9g)
1	Cold Pack	2		4" x 5" (10x125 cm)
1	CPR Breathing Barrier	1		
1	Eye/Skin Wash	1		1fl oz (29.6 ml) total
2	Eye Covering	2		2.9" sq (19 sq cm)
1	First Aid Guide	1		
1	Foil Blanket	1		52" x 84" (132x213 cm)
10	Hand Sanitizer	20		1/32 oz (0.9g)
4	Medical Exam Gloves	8		
1	Roller Bandage	2		2" x 4" yd (5 cm x 3.66 m)
1	Scissors	1		
2	Sterile Pad	4		3" x 3" (7.5 x 7.5 cm)
2	Trauma Pad	4		5" x 9" (12.7 x 22.9 cm)
1	Triangular Bandage	2		40" x 40" x 56" (101x101x142 cm)
		1	Tourniquet	
		1	Scissors	
		1	Splint	4" x 24" (10.2 x 61 cm)

ANSI/ISEAZ308-2021 – Standards for Workplace First Aid Kits

Class A: intended to provide a basic range of products to deal with most common types of injuries encountered in the workplace.

Examples include major wounds, minor wounds (cuts & abrasion), Minor burns, and eye injuries.

Class B: intended to provide a broader range & quantity of supplies to deal with injuries personal may encounter in more populated, complex, and/or high-risk environments.

Fallacy: I have hand sanitizer.

Hand sanitizer is a remarkable product; however, it is commonly misused and mishandled, especially during the recent COVID pandemic. It is an alcohol-based gel antiseptic designed for situations when water is unavailable. A significant issue with hand sanitizer is the misconception that it is sufficient in preventing germs. It is not suitable for use on dirty, soiled, or greasy hands, limiting its effectiveness in various scenarios where it is promoted (e.g., military, sports, & outdoor activities). Health experts consistently advise washing hands with soap and water as the preferred method, rather than relying solely on hand sanitizer.

Hand sanitizers are marketed as having the ability to eliminate up to 99% of germs, which is indeed accurate. However, their efficacy is influenced by various factors including the amount used, duration of exposure, frequency of use, and application technique. Furthermore, the effectiveness of hand sanitizers is contingent upon whether the specific germs or bacteria are susceptible to the product. It is important to note that not all hand sanitizers are created equal, and counterfeit products have become more widespread, especially during the pandemic. It is crucial to be aware that hand sanitizers are not effective against encysted parasites like Giardia, a significant concern for military personnel and individuals who spend time outdoors. Additionally, they are ineffective against nonenveloped viruses and bacterial spores.

The U.S. Center for Disease Control and World Health Organization have raised concerns about the use of Hand Sanitizer due to its flammability and potential risks associated with ingestion. Despite being highly beneficial in settings with low hand washing compliance, such as schools and unsanitary environments, there are alcohol-free alternatives that have proven to be equally effective. It is recommended that Hand Sanitizers are utilized as a complement to regular hygiene practices, like hand washing, or as a last resort in emergency situations, rather than being the primary method of sanitization.

Lie: Space blankets are useless.

The Space blanket, also known as Thermal blankets or emergency blankets, are a highly practical tool used in various situations, particularly those involving disasters and survival. Despite some critics in the industry claiming that space blankets are ineffective, it is likely that they have encountered low-quality counterfeit products flooding the market. This innovative product has been a lifesaver for military medical personnel who often face hypothermia in harsh conditions. By reflecting the body heat back to the person, space blankets serve their purpose effectively. Although they may be perceived as uncomfortable, flimsy, and noisy, they are undeniably useful. Regardless of the manufacturer, the product functions as intended. Cheaper manufacturing processes may result in less durability, but not in reduced effectiveness. Moreover, space blankets offer versatility, such as being used for shelter construction or as a fire reflector. Their compact size makes them easy to carry, making them a must-have item, especially for medics who can now carry multiple blankets instead of just one traditional blanket.

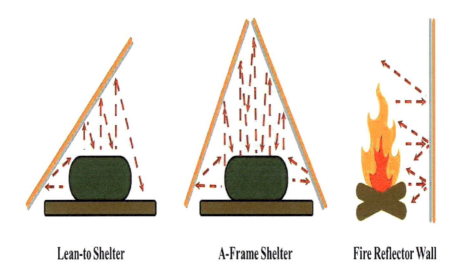

Lean-to Shelter   A-Frame Shelter   Fire Reflector Wall

Fallacy: Drinking alcohol will warm you up.

Some people are under the impression that consuming alcohol can help warm the body and assist in combating hypothermia. However, alcohol does not actually raise body temperature. Instead, it creates a sensation of warmth. Those who drink alcohol may perceive themselves as being warmer or may become less sensitive to feeling cold. Additionally, alcohol dulls the senses, leading individuals to believe they are not cold even though the environment is still impacting their body.

An advantage is that small amounts can help maintain a person's morale, but the problem of overexposure needs to be dealt with eventually. Additionally, alcohol can serve other purposes for survival such as providing fuel for cooking, disinfecting wounds, sterilizing medical tools, and soothing nerves when used moderately.

Fallacy: Urinating on Athletes foot.

One common folk remedy that occasionally surfaces, often linked to sports or the military, involves the belief that urinating on someone's Athlete's foot can treat it. Athlete's foot, also known as Tinea Pedis, is a fungal infection that commonly affects the feet, typically starting between the toes due to sweaty feet in tightly enclosed shoes. It is characterized by a scaly rash, itching, and redness, and can be transmitted through contact with contaminated floors, towels, or clothing. Despite preventive measures, some individuals appear to be more prone to contracting it than others.

The remedy is believed to have originated from the concept that urine contains "urea," which is used in high concentrations to treat fungal infections. However, urologists argue that this remedy is ineffective, as the amount of "urea" present in urine is insufficient to cure the infection.

Myth: Urinate on a jellyfish sting.

Several research studies have been conducted on this matter, and none have demonstrated any advantages. A number of these studies have indicated that doing so can actually trigger more venom, resulting in increased pain. The concept of painful jellyfish stings has also led to the misconception that all jellyfish can sting a person. However, not all species of jellyfish can sting. The most common jellyfish stings come from the Bluebottle found along the eastern coastline of Australia. Many beaches have jellyfish at certain times of the year that pose no threat of stinging a person.

The most efficient advice is to eliminate the stingers by rinsing them with sea water. Using fresh water may trigger venom. Avoid rubbing the affected area as this may also activate the venom cells left by the stinger. Ensure the stingers are removed without direct contact. Once the stingers have been removed, hot water (104 -113°F) can be used to either rinse or soak the wound. Vinegar, which contains acidic acid, can be applied to the cleaned site to alleviate pain. Calamine lotion, hydrocortisone cream, and ice packs are also beneficial. Some beaches have vinegar solution stations available in areas with a high risk of jellyfish stings.

Myth: Rub frostbitten skin.

The concept of massaging frostbitten skin has been discussed for numerous years. It is instinctual for individuals to desire to rub their chilly extremities, however, engaging in such action under frostbite conditions can lead to harm. When skin is frostbitten, ice crystals can develop and cause harm to tissues and blood vessels if rubbed. It is advisable to refrain from rubbing whenever feasible, and treatment for frostbite should only be administered when there is no possibility of the affected area becoming frostbitten again.

Myth: Rub snow on frostbite.

A persistent myth is the belief that rubbing snow on frostbitten skin is beneficial. The rationale behind this notion is that frostbitten limbs should be rewarmed gradually to avoid severe tissue damage. However, this practice was debunked in the 1950s. The continued prevalence of this myth can be attributed to the popularity of older documents, literature, and books that promote it. Additionally, the field of medical and first aid practices in survival situations remains one of the least researched areas for survivalists and preppers. Many experts in disaster preparedness and survival do not critically evaluate the effectiveness of traditional first aid methods, often directing individuals to seek guidance from the medical community, which emphasizes contemporary techniques rather than assessing the validity of historical practices.

Myth: Frostbite and/or hypothermia only happens when it's cold outside.

Frostbite and hypothermia can begin as soon as the body temperature falls below the normal level of 98°F, regardless of the external temperature. The severity of these conditions is determined by how much the body temperature decreases and the duration it remains below 98°F. Additionally, factors such as moisture, wind conditions, and the individual's clothing can either exacerbate or mitigate the risk of developing these ailments.

Myth: Hypothermia kills you within minutes of falling into freezing water.

When individuals fall into freezing water, drowning typically occurs within minutes. Panic often sets in, leading to inhalation of water, submersion, and sometimes slipping beneath the ice, resulting in a failure to resurface. It is important to recognize that the body instinctively reacts to the cold by gasping, which frequently causes individuals to choke on water. This involuntary gasp can trigger a state of panic. If a person does not succumb immediately due to panic or inability to swim, hypothermia can take up to 30 minutes to become fatal. Experts advise that when falling into freezing water, individuals should focus on calming themselves and aim to exit the water within 10 minutes. After this period, the cold significantly impairs mobility. If escape is not possible, a person can remain afloat for up to an hour before losing consciousness, and those equipped with flotation devices may have an increased chance of survival.

Fallacy: Depictions of drowning victims in media.

The media often portrays dramatic narratives of drowning victims being saved by CPR, but the issue lies in the unrealistic depiction of immediate recovery and individuals simply walking it off. This misrepresentation leads to a lack of awareness regarding the potential dangers of drowning-related illnesses and injuries. It is important to note that the correct term is near drowning, as drowning implies death. Those who have experienced near drowning are still at risk of various health complications such as brain damage, lung issues, heart problems, and electrolyte imbalances. Therefore, it is crucial for anyone involved in such incidents to seek medical attention promptly, even if they feel fine.

Fallacy: Oxygenated Kiss:

The concept of the oxygenate kiss, often portrayed as dramatic and romantic in the media, is a misconception. Studies on mouth-to-mouth resuscitation suggest that only about 16% of oxygen is transferred from one person to another. While performing this act may temporarily delay the drowning process, it is more effective to remove the victim from the water.

Individuals who are alert and aware will actively resist the involuntary inhalation of air to prevent the drowning reflex from kicking in. This method is ineffective on an unconscious individual, as their lungs will simply fill with water, and attempting mouth-to-mouth resuscitation will only force air into their water-filled lungs. Mouth-to-mouth resuscitation often succeeds because an unconscious person out of the water does not have the body's natural defense mechanisms in place and is able to accept most of the forced air. Numerous studies have indicated that mouth-to-mouth resuscitation is not very effective, which is why emergency medical services (EMS) provide supplemental oxygen to ensure the provision of oxygen.

Fallacy: Do not remove impaled objects.

It is generally advised not to remove an impaled object, but there are exceptions to this rule. The decision may vary based on factors such as the specific situation, the injured person's knowledge, or the expertise of the person providing treatment. Someone with a good understanding of anatomy and wound care may be able to safely remove the object, especially if it is in a certain location. Whether or not to remove the object also depends on how quickly medical help can be accessed - if immediate medical attention is available, it is best to wait for professional assistance. However, if there is a delay in reaching medical care, removing the object may be necessary to ensure the person's survival.

Items located near the heart, eye, or head should only be extracted by medical professionals within a medical setting. Those lacking medical expertise or a proper grasp of anatomy and physiology should refrain from removing any impaled objects. It is advisable to secure the object in place to prevent movement and seek medical attention promptly.

Fallacy: shaking off the choking.

The portrayal of choking situations in the media often misrepresents the proper medical technique for dislodging a foreign body from the airway. Abdominal thrust, also known as the (Hi.... Maneuver), is the standard term used by medical professionals to describe this method.

The media often portrays a scenario where someone is choking, and another person comes to the rescue by performing abdominal thrusts to expel the food, making it seem like a foolproof method. However, the reality is that many individuals may lose consciousness before the food is dislodged, requiring the need for CPR. Whether the food is removed through abdominal thrusts or CPR, choking victims can still face similar issues as near drowning, such as brain injury, lung complications, and cardiac problems. Additionally, the use of abdominal thrust techniques can lead to internal injuries, especially if performed by someone who is not properly trained or is under distress.

Fallacy: CPR representation.

Cardiopulmonary resuscitation (CPR) is a highly effective intervention, but its effectiveness is contingent upon several other factors being in place. For CPR to be effective, it must be combined with defibrillation (electrical shock) and advanced medications/procedures. Essentially, CPR serves as a temporary measure, prolonging the negative effects without resolving the underlying issue. According to a study, the survivability rate with advanced healthcare and CPR was 80%, while CPR and defibrillation alone resulted in a survivability rate of 40%, and CPR technique alone had a survivability rate of 25-30%. This indicates that the chances of survival with CPR alone are not very high. The survivability rate of 25-30% highlights the discrepancy between media portrayal and the reality of CPR.

In the survival context, there is a widespread misconception regarding the use of CPR. The majority of CPR and first aid literature in survival scenarios is of poor quality. These publications simply repeat the same information without providing proper context. The reality is that the longer CPR is performed, the less likely it is to result in a positive outcome. Therefore, discussing CPR in the context of survival is futile, as most survival literature emphasizes the concept of needing to wait three days or longer to be rescued. For CPR to be effective, the patient must reach a hospital as quickly as possible (ideally within 10 minutes) and have access to defibrillation and advanced medical care without delay.

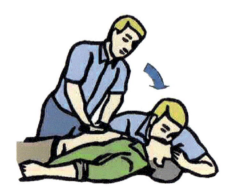

Three exceptions exist. CPR performed due to airway obstruction from a foreign object, near drowning, and lightning strikes typically yield positive results. If someone is administering CPR to a victim of a heart attack or stroke, they should not be surprised if CPR is unsuccessful. However, if the person was struck by lightning, experienced near drowning, or lost consciousness due to choking on a foreign object, then CPR is strongly advised.

Myth: Defibrillators restart the heart.

The heart relies on an electrical signal to maintain its function. This signal is crucial for establishing the heart's rhythm. When a heart monitor is attached to a patient, it detects this electrical activity. A defibrillator does not revive a heart that lacks an electrical signal; instead, it aims to restore a normal rhythm from an abnormal one through electrical shocks. Automatic external defibrillators (AEDs), commonly found in public areas, can only identify two types of abnormal signals, while hospital defibrillators display the signal pattern, allowing medical professionals to assess the specific type of abnormality. A prevalent misconception perpetuated by the media is the notion of shocking a "flat line." In reality, asystole, or the "flat line," is not a condition that can be treated with shocks, and attempting to do so may complicate the situation for medical personnel. Asystole requires alternative medical interventions.

Myth: Loss 50-80% of body heat through your head.

It is probable that this misconception originated from military experiments conducted in the 1950s. The belief stems from the fact that heat dissipates from the body through any exposed area. Even during winter, individuals tend to bundle up, covering most of their body and leaving only the head exposed for heat to escape. The heat in other parts of the body can also be retained by layers of clothing and radiated back to the body. Historically, headgear technology was lacking compared to other clothing, resulting in a greater heat loss, but it has since caught up. Additionally, hair plays a role in trapping heat around the head. The absence of headgear and the common practice of short or shaved heads in early military studies likely contributed to the origin of this myth.

Pathways of Heat Loss

Skin *(Major pathway)*	**Radiation & Conduction** – Heat is lost from the body to cooler air objects
	Convection – Air currents move warm air away from the skin.
	Sweating – excess body heat evaporates sweat on the skin surface
Respiratory Tract *(secondary pathway)*	**Evaporation** – Body heat evaporates sweat on the skin surface
Urinary Tract *(Minor Pathway)*	**Urination** – Urine is a body temperature when eliminated
Digestive Tract *(Minor Pathway)*	**Defecation** – Feces are at the body temperature when eliminated

Lie: Let hypothermic victims sleep it off.

It is imperative that an individual experiencing hypothermia is not permitted to sleep unsupervised in a medical setting. Sleeping can cause crucial body systems responsible for generating heat to shut down, further complicating the condition. Maintaining wakefulness may prove challenging due to fatigue being a common symptom of hypothermia. Additionally, it is crucial to refrain from providing alcohol or tobacco to a hypothermic patient as these substances can impede the rewarming process.

Myth: "snuggling for hypothermia"

Discussion of hypothermia treatment in challenging environments often includes the unconventional method of placing two unclothed individuals in a sleeping bag to assist in warming a hypothermic patient. While there is limited research to support its effectiveness, studies have also indicated that it does not cause harm to the patient. Ideally, both individuals should be unclothed or at least wearing minimal clothing, as garments can impede heat transfer. The use of a mylar blanket is more effective than using another person.

Lie: Catch a snake for identification.

It is unnecessary to catch the snake for identification after a snake bite. Trying to capture the snake may lead to more people getting bitten, resulting in an increased number of patients and a higher demand for snake venom. Furthermore, medical personnel are not equipped to handle live snakes brought to them. The best course of action is to provide a detailed description of the snake to medical staff, who are likely familiar with the venomous snakes in the area or can contact the necessary authorities for identification. In addition, a photo can be taken using a smartphone with a zoom feature, which is commonly available nowadays.

Myth: Sucking out the venom from a snake bite.

Once again, the media has misrepresented this concept for dramatic effect, perpetuating the dangerous myth that someone must suck out the poison from a snake bite in order to save the victim. The effectiveness of this technique is highly debated, with multiple contradicting studies. What is not debatable is how the technique is more dangerous for the individual performing the sucking than the potential effectiveness for the victim. It is widely advised by numerous sources that the victim should try to remain as calm as possible in order to lower their heart rate, which will prevent the venom from spreading rapidly through the bloodstream. Some sources also suggest using a two-inch constricting band to slow down the venom's spread, although other sources dispute its effectiveness as the venom can still spread through the tissue. Almost every source advises against attempting to suck out the venom. Those who advocate for suction devices are typically affiliated with the company selling the product, and there is very little independent research that has proven their effectiveness.

IF A SNAKE BITE YOU

DO

Stay calm

Remove shoes and jewelry; swelling will occur

Reposition so bite is at or below the heart level

Head to a hospital ASAP and be prepared to describe the snake.

DON'T

Panic

Cut the wound

Try to suck out the venom

Apply an arterial tourniquet or ice

Drink any alcohol or caffeine

Wash the bite

Try to capture the snake

Fallacy: Tampons for bullet holes

One approach to treating battlefield gunshot wounds involves placing a tampon into the wound. This method has its pros and cons. At one time, it was a practical but limited option for treating wounds. Medical personnel dealing with gunshot wounds were constrained by the amount of supplies they could carry and the available options for medical treatment, including availability and transportation. The tampon was a convenient choice, as it contained a variety of quick and effective wound treatment supplies that required minimal space and were not burdensome to carry. It could also be easily stowed in a pocket when carrying a medical bag was impractical.

Currently, this is not a favorable choice. Combat gauze, for instance, is advantageous due to its compact packaging, allowing for more to be carried while occupying less space in a medical bag. Moreover, combat gauze is treated with a special process that assists in blood clotting. Compression gauze, on the other hand, is stored in vacuum-sealed containers to minimize space consumption and is made of materials that are more effective than tampons. One drawback of tampons is that they are now made from a different material compared to the previous version, which does not interact with the wound in the same way as the older, thicker material. If you must carry one for any reason, ensure it is the type that can absorb a significant amount.

Tampons can be a valuable addition to medical kits due to their intended purposes, effectiveness in managing nose bleeds, and suitability for basic wound packing. Moreover, they offer various alternative survival applications like serving as fire tender or a makeshift water filter.

The myth's widespread belief is often seen as an inside joke within military and emergency medical circles. While a medic may humorously reference it to share insider knowledge, the presence of a tampon in their kit serves a different purpose altogether.

Myth: Rub Butter, oil, Windex, or other such things on burns.

Over the years, numerous remedies have been suggested for treating burns, with a variety of objects recommended by individuals. Common suggestions include butter and oil, while less conventional options like Windex and mustard have also been mentioned. However, none of these substances provide any genuine healing benefits. While they may offer temporary relief from pain by creating a barrier that blocks exposed pain receptors from the air, they can also contaminate the wound and increase the risk of infection. Even ice is not advisable, as it merely numbs the pain temporarily without addressing the underlying issue.

For proper wound care, it is essential to clean the area with mild soap and water, dry it thoroughly, and then cover it with a sterile dressing. Additionally, it is important to avoid the common misconception of popping blisters, as they serve as the body's natural defense mechanism, providing insulation to the injury. Rupturing blisters can lead to infections and hinder the healing process.

Fallacy: Do not let those with a head injury fall asleep.

It was previously thought that allowing someone with a head injury to fall asleep could result in them never waking up. However, this belief has been debunked, except in cases of severe head trauma. Sleep is essential for the healing process. If an individual is awake and conversing normally, it generally indicates that the internal damage is minor. Signs such as altered mental status, pinpoint pupils, slurred speech, or other abnormal indicators suggest more significant injury. For anyone with a head injury, it is advisable to keep them awake until they can be evaluated by a medical professional. This precaution is crucial because individuals with head injuries who appear drowsy may create misleading impressions during assessments. Additionally, assessing a person's mental state is challenging if they are asleep. If medical personnel are unaware that the individual has fallen asleep, they might mistakenly interpret this as a sign of unconsciousness, which is a more serious indication of injury.

If you believe the injury is not serious, you can monitor the individual overnight for any indications of deterioration, such as difficulty breathing, a weak pulse, or unresponsiveness. Some healthcare professionals suggest waking them every few hours during the initial nights to ask straightforward questions and assess whether their condition appears normal or if there are any changes in behavior. Gradually extend the intervals between wakeups each night, provided the person remains stable. If you notice any differences, it is important to seek medical assistance.

Rousing individuals who have sustained concussions may extend the duration of their symptoms. Additionally, awakening those with a history of multiple concussions can lead to intense headaches, as well as difficulties with mood and cognitive function.

Fallacy: Only hydrate with water when suffering from diarrhea.

In cases of diarrhea, individuals are often advised to stick to drinking water in order to prevent dehydration caused by fluid loss. This recommendation stems from the observation that people tend to opt for beverages like coffee, tea, and alcohol over water. Many of these common beverages act as diuretics, exacerbating dehydration. The last thing someone suffering from dehydration needs is to consume a beverage that further depletes their body's fluids. As a result, it has become common practice to suggest sticking to water only. However, a drawback of this approach is that individuals with diarrhea are also losing essential electrolytes.

Previously, electrolyte solutions were sold as medical and first aid supplies, but nowadays there are various electrolyte beverages commonly marketed as "sports drinks." It is advisable to consume electrolyte drinks alongside water. Sports drinks should be diluted due to their high sugar content. A recommended ratio is 3 parts water to 1 part drink. Pedialyte has gained popularity in the military for its hydration benefits, as it has minimal sugar and is rich in electrolytes. Moreover, Pedialyte is more enjoyable to drink compared to plain water.

6 MAIN ELECTROLYTES IN THE BODY

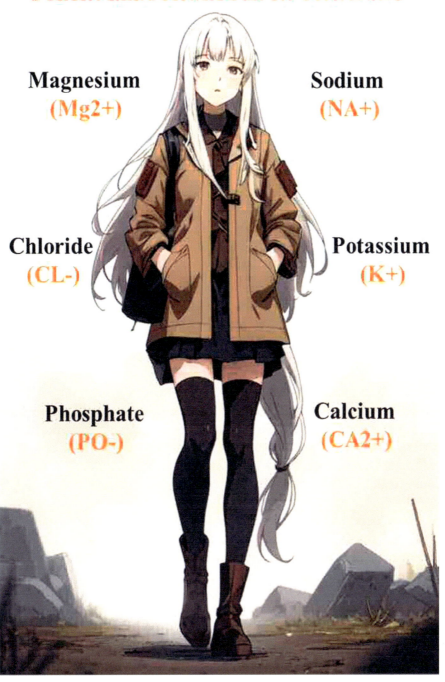

Magnesium
(Mg2+)

Sodium
(NA+)

Chloride
(CL-)

Potassium
(K+)

Phosphate
(PO-)

Calcium
(CA2+)

Fallacy: Surgical mask/bandanas spreading disease:

Using surgical masks, cloth, or bandanas to prevent the spread of disease is not a myth. The concept is more complex than some people realize. Wearing some form of face covering helps to stop the transmission of disease through airborne particles. This concept is particularly effective in preventing the spread of illness when the infected person (vector) wears a mask, which prevents the virus from spreading through coughing, sneezing, or breathing.

The choice of face covering is also a determining factor. The material of the face covering plays a crucial role in whether disease particles can pass through, either from the outside in or from the inside out, depending on the size of the particles.

Note: At the present moment, there is a significant debate surrounding the efficacy of masks. Despite being confronted with substantial evidence, some people will continue to debate in favor of or against wearing them. It is ultimately up to each individual to decide whether or not to wear a mask based on their beliefs. Below are some established facts to consider.

Cloth masks provide some level of protection, although not as effective as medical masks. The effectiveness of surgical masks is still a topic of debate, while N95 respirator masks are considered the most beneficial. It's important to note that other types of masks, like paint respirators, are not designed for disease prevention and may even cause health issues for the wearer.

Wearing a mask does not compromise your immune system. The strength of the immune system is determined by its response to pathogens like diseases, bacteria, viruses, etc., as well as individual factors such as health, lifestyle, and exposure. The topic of the immune system is intricate and could fill entire books on its own.

If an individual opts to wear a mask for disease prevention, it is essential that they cover the entire mouth and nose. Leaving any part of the mouth or nose exposed creates an opportunity for a vector to enter the body. Single-use masks should only be worn once, as they are not intended for repeated use. Other types of masks that can be washed should be laundered daily for hygiene purposes and to help prevent other health issues. Note that repeated laundering of the mask with break down the material allowing for greater sized pathogens to eventually make it through the mask and into your system.

Myth: Rusty metal causes tetanus.

It was a common belief in the past that getting a wound from a rusty object, particularly a rusty nail, would lead to Tetanus, also known as "Lockjaw." Tetanus is a bacterial infection that results in muscle spasms, fever, and difficulty swallowing in all instances. It can be fatal in 10% of cases. Contrary to popular belief, Tetanus is caused by bacteria found in soil and feces, not by rust. This misconception stems from the high number of individuals, such as cowboys and homesteaders, who contracted Tetanus in the past due to injuries sustained during field work. While Tetanus was a significant concern in earlier times, advancements in modern medicine have made it a manageable condition.

Fallacy: Brush your teeth after every meal.

For many years, children have been instructed to brush their teeth before each meal. However, dentists have found that excessive brushing can lead to the erosion of tooth enamel. Most dentists advise brushing twice a day using the proper technique and fluoride toothpaste.

The recommended brushing method involves starting with the outer surfaces, holding the brush at a 45-degree angle, and using circular motions. For the inner surfaces, tilt the brush horizontally and move it up and down along the teeth. It is important to gently brush the gums and conclude by brushing the tongue. It is advisable to brush for about two minutes and to floss once daily. Replace your toothbrush every three months or when the bristles become frayed.

Fallacy: Medication Expirations.

It is crucial to pay attention to medication expirations to ensure the most effective product, especially in emergency medical situations. While medications do not suddenly become ineffective on the day of expiration, their strength may decrease as some, or all parts of the medication begin to break down. For over-the-counter drugs, this may not be a significant issue, but for emergency drugs, a lack of strength can be life-threatening. According to a joint study by the Federal Drug Administration and Department of Defense, nearly 90% of the drugs tested were still effective after expiration, with some lasting up to fifteen years.

Research indicates that solid pill forms of medication tend to retain the highest stability post-expiration dates. Certain medications have the potential to harbor harmful bacterial growth once expired. Antibiotics are known to pose risks after expiration, as they may become less effective, leading to the development of resistant strains of bacteria. Additionally, some antibiotics can transform into poisonous substances shortly after their expiration date. Studies have identified insulin, liquid medications requiring refrigeration, eye drops, injectables, medications with biologic components (such as blood plasma), and specially compounded medications as the most high-risk options for use after expiration.

Fallacy: people get sick in winter because of the cold.

The occurrence of illness is not directly related to temperature. Instead, the prevalence of sickness during winter months is primarily due to viruses. Colder temperatures tend to drive individuals indoors, resulting in closer proximity to one another. This increased indoor interaction facilitates the spread of viruses, leading to a higher incidence of the common cold during the winter season.

Lie: Tourniquets as a last resort:

The Committee for Tactical Combat Casualty Care was established during the Iraq war to conduct research on the most preventable causes of death on the battlefield and how to mitigate them. One significant finding from the study was the effectiveness of tourniquets in preventing life-threatening bleeding. Over the years, the committee has consistently demonstrated the life-saving benefits of tourniquets. Additionally, they have debunked misconceptions about the dangers of tourniquets, proving them to be either exaggerated or baseless.

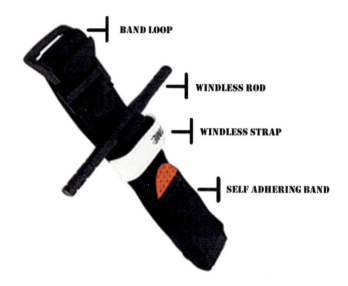

BAND LOOP

WINDLESS ROD

WINDLESS STRAP

SELF ADHERING BAND

My personal investigation revealed that the concept of tourniquets as a "last resort" was documented as early as the civil war, when a surgeon expressed concerns that they were causing more harm than good and were being used by incompetent individuals. The early opposition to tourniquet use stemmed from the initial design of early tourniquets, which were either bulky and complex devices requiring specific knowledge for proper use and an ideal patient positioning, or simple straps. Today, tourniquets have been proven to be not only effective but also a leading tool in trauma care. Those who still advocate for tourniquets as a last resort either rely on outdated sources for medical knowledge or hold an ego-driven concept of what a layman (and sometimes medic) is capable of.

Although the assertion that "use as a last resort" is incorrect, there are certain risks linked to the utilization of a tourniquet that individuals must be aware of, including the necessity for proper training in its application, understanding when to use it, and ensuring it is used appropriately. Despite its seemingly simple nature, a tourniquet is a medical tool that should be handled with the same level of care and respect as any other medical device to avoid potential consequences.

Common Tourniquet Errors

X	**NOT** using one when you should or waiting too long to put it on
X	**NOT** pulling all the slack out before tightening
X	**NOT** making it tight enough – the TQ should stop the bleeding **AND** eliminate the distal pulse
X	**NOT** using a second TQ, if needed
X	Using a TQ for minimal bleeding (however, **when in doubt**, apply a TQ)
X	Putting it on too proximally if the bleeding site is clearly visible
X	Loosening TQs for a period to allow recirculation of a limb
X	Taking a TQ off **Prematurely** when it is still needed for hemorrhage control.
X	**DON'T** put TQs over joints!

Fallacy: Use a belt as a Torniquet.

There is a specific scenario often depicted in media where an individual is shot in an extremity and manages to save their life heroically by using a belt as a tourniquet. While using a belt to stop a life-threatening bleed in an extremity can help reduce blood loss, it is not as effective as other methods. The key factor in the effectiveness of modern tourniquets is the use of a windlass (the dowel-shaped stick). Without a windlass, the band cannot completely stop the blood flow to the extent necessary to save a life. If a material other than a commercial tourniquet is being used, it must be strong enough to withstand the pressure exerted by the turning of the windlass and flexible enough to conform to the limb it is applied to. Materials like cotton or synthetic fibers, ranging from two to four inches, are ideal for adaptability. On the other hand, materials like leather or web belting can bunch up as the windlass is turned, making them less effective. It is not recommended to use materials smaller than two inches, as they can cause damage to the limb and may not effectively stop the bleeding. Any material can be used to make a windlass, but it must be secured after placement to maintain pressure. Prior to the commercialization of tourniquets during the Global War on Terrorism, the most effective tourniquet was a homemade device created by military medical personnel. This device consisted of "old school" green triangle bandages and a wooden windlass, typically made from a branch or stick.

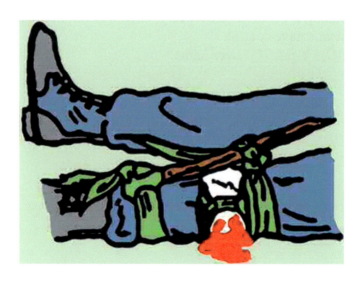

CHAPTER EIGHT:
NAVIGATION, MOVEMENT, & SIGNALING

Chapter Eight: Navigation, Movement, And Signaling

Fallacy: Follow the stream or river to safety.

The concept of relying on a stream or river for safety is an ancient practice that was once practical but presents challenges in today's world. In the past, humans rarely strayed from established routes near water sources. However, with modern transportation like airplanes, trains, and cars, people can travel great distances away from populated areas. As a result, individuals often become lost in remote locations where following a water source may lead to safety or further isolation. Safety along water sources can be many miles apart.

Fallacy: I can yell for help.

In a survival situation, a person can face difficulties when trying to yell for help. The ability for sound to travel depends on various factors, such as the environment and obstructions. Yelling and screaming can also lead to voice burnout, especially for those under distress. It is recommended to carry a whistle designed for survival or distress situations, as it can be more effective than yelling. Different whistles have different capabilities, so it's important to choose one specifically designed for survival or distress.

Fallacy: Using rope as a safety line.

There are two situations in which a rope is utilized as a safety line. One situation involves securing the rope around the waist while attempting to cross water bodies. Two issues with a safety line in water bodies are that the rope can get tangled on objects or even the person while swimming. The other issue is related to having another person at the opposite end of the rope. This individual can create complications by either losing grip of the rope or pulling the rope at an unsuitable moment.

The safety line serves another purpose, which is for climbing. If the safety line is not tied properly, it can lead to serious injuries if the climber falls. Additionally, the safety line can get tangled, causing minor issues or even putting the climber in danger if not handled carefully.

When multiple people are tied together during climbs or hikes, improper use of the ropes can result in dragging others down. This is why professional climbers use break devices that attach to the rope at intervals, so that if someone falls, the device will catch them before they pull on others, giving them a chance to prepare for the fall or take some form of action.

Myth: escape for a deserted island.

In certain disasters, like boating accidents, a person may become stranded on a deserted island. The term "deserted" refers to an island without any human inhabitants, not necessarily devoid of all life. The media often sensationalizes stories of people ending up on deserted islands due to plane crashes, but the likelihood of this happening is low due to flight paths. If someone does find themselves on a deserted island, it is statistically safer to stay put and wait for help, assuming there is enough food and water available. While the media may depict individuals building rafts to escape, it is extremely challenging to navigate the sea in a raft, especially considering the obstacles like barrier reefs and strong tidal flows that can make it dangerous to venture out to sea from the island.

Fallacy: Using moss to find directions.

The concept of using moss placement to determine direction is an ancient method that is only accurate under specific conditions and in limited geographical regions. The belief is that the north side of a tree, receiving less sunlight due to the sun's position, will have more moss growth on its south side. However, this idea is flawed because moss growth is influenced by factors like moisture, shade, and tree canopy density. Additionally, this method is most applicable in forested areas, as moss can thrive in swamps but is unlikely to be found in deserts. In dense jungle vegetation, moss is abundant and may be challenging to locate.

Lie: change voicemail with details.

Social media has recently popularized the concept of a "life hack" suggesting that if a person is lost, they should update their voicemail to ask for help with details of their situation. However, most "life hacks" found on the internet are often misleading, impractical, or even dangerous. While there is a slim chance that someone might hear the message and get help, the reality is that many people no longer check their voicemails regularly. In times of distress, the caller tends to hang up immediately upon hearing the voicemail prompt, hoping to reach the person directly. If someone is unable to connect with emergency services like 911, it is unlikely that they will be able to update their voicemail message.

Smartphones also repeatedly attempt to connect to cell towers, which can drain the battery with each attempt. The phone will continue to do so until it runs out of power. Not only does the phone's internal system drain the battery faster, but each attempt to change the voicemail will also deplete the battery. To conserve battery, it is recommended to switch the phone to airplane mode and only attempt to text or call every few hours.

One possible solution is to try sending a text message with details of your situation to a trusted person. Text messages have been known to be delivered even when the phone indicates no service. Another option is to wait until you are in a higher location, such as a hilltop, cliff, or mountain. Sometimes a signal can be received at a higher elevation. Individuals should be cautious not to injure themselves while trying to climb to a higher location. It is advised that individuals do not climb trees to reach higher ground.

Fallacy: The NorthStar does not move.

One of the oldest beliefs is that the north star remains stationary. Despite this, the north star does indeed move; it is the people's perception that remains unchanged. Polaris, also known as the North Star, sits directly above the Earth's northern axis, causing the sky to appear as though it is rotating around the position of the north star. Even though the star may appear to move slightly in a person's perception, its movement is so minimal that it is imperceptible to the naked eye.

Locating Polaris can be challenging due to the need to find specific constellations as reference points. As the sky shifts throughout the year, individuals must be able to identify certain constellations to easily locate the star. To find the north star, one must first locate the Big Dipper and draw an imaginary line through the two stars that form the outer edge of the cup. Follow this line until it reaches the star at the end of the handle of the Little Dipper.

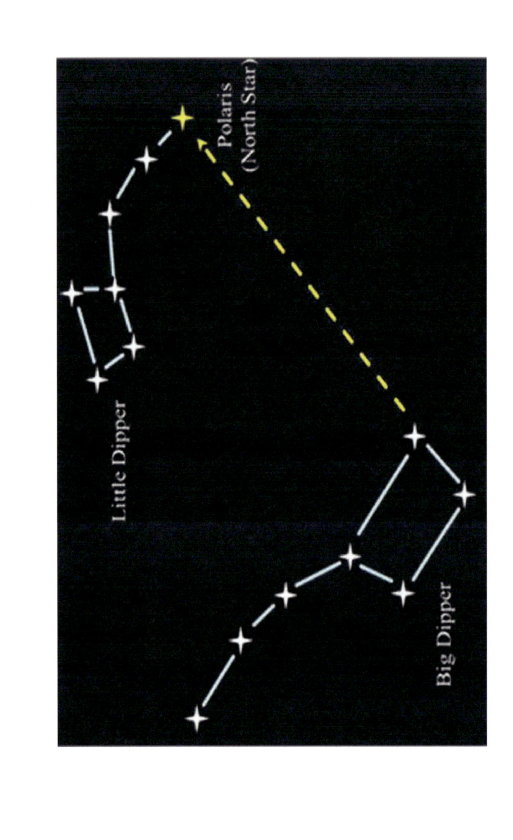

Lie: SOS means Save our ship/soul:

SOS is the acronym linked to a particular series of sounds in Morse Code. Morse code is a global system of sounds connected to the alphabet, comprising of combinations of dots and dashes corresponding to each letter. The SOS signal comprises of a series of three dots, three dashes, and three dots. This specific sequence was established by the international radio telegraphic convention in 1906 to symbolize distress due to its simplicity in identification during usage.

Subsequently, mainstream culture began linking it to different shortened versions of phrases, with the most prevalent ones being "save our ship" or "save our soul". The perception of it being an acronym stems from the extensive use of acronyms in the military.

SOS gained widespread recognition for its association with distress signals, leading to the adoption of the letters SOS in different contexts to indicate distress. For instance, distress can be conveyed by spelling out SOS using rocks, or by displaying the letters SOS through printing or painting. Additionally, variations involving the three dots, dash, dot pattern have gained popularity as alternative distress signals, including the use of short and long flashes of light or short and long blasts of sound.

American	International		American	International		American	International
A		M		1	
Á		N		2	
Ä		Ñ		3	
Å		O		4	
B		Ö		5	
C		P		6	
CH		Q		7	
D		R		8	
E		S		9	
É		T		0	
F		U		&	
G		Ü			
H		V			
I		W			
J		X			
K		Y			
L		Z			

Myth: Swim parallel to shore if caught in rip current.

One debunked myth is the notion that when caught in a rip current, a person should swim parallel to the shore. It was widely believed that the rip current would pull the individual underwater, leading to panic and a desperate attempt to swim closer to shore. This would result in exhaustion from fighting the current, ultimately leading to drowning. However, the truth is that the rip current actually pulls the individual out to sea, and going underwater is more related to panic, improper swimming, and the force of the waves.

Swimming parallel to the shore was advised in order to escape the rip current, followed by swimming back to the shore. The issue arose from the lack of understanding until recently that the rip current is accompanied by a feeder current, which essentially runs alongside the edge of the rip current and pushes back into it. Consequently, anyone approaching the edge of the rip current would also have to contend with the feeder current, leading to the same set of challenges.

It has been proven false that a person can be pulled all the way out to sea by a rip current. Instead, the current will only drag them a sufficient distance to make the return swim difficult and painful.

There is much debate in scientific circles about the best course of action. Nevertheless, one effective approach for dealing with a mild rip current is to float along with it in a circular pattern. By doing so, you may be brought closer to the shore or to a point where swimming will be easier. It's important to note that this method is not applicable to rip currents that occur during storms, as these are more likely to either pull a person under due to their strong force or carry them far out to sea.

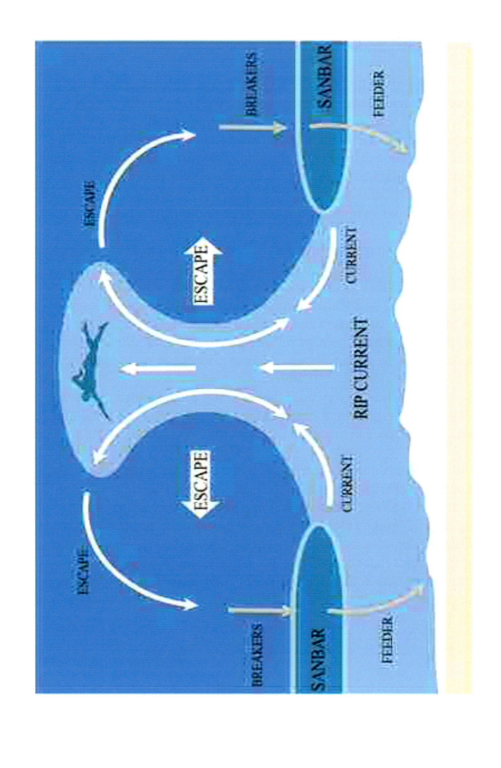

Myth: Wait 30 minutes before swimming.

One of the enduring myths that has persisted through the years is the notion that individuals should wait half an hour after a meal before swimming to avoid the risk of cramping up and drowning. This belief stemmed from the idea that eating would cause a shift in blood flow from the limbs to the stomach for digestion, potentially leading to cramping if the limbs were used too soon. However, there is no significant alteration in blood flow between the limbs and the digestive system. Cramping while swimming is more likely due to factors like dehydration, heat-related illnesses, or overworked muscles

Fallacy: Can not get lost with a GPS.

The GPS, or global positioning satellite, is considered one of the most significant inventions of the 20th century. However, despite its widespread use through smartphones, thousands of people still manage to get lost every day. This is because GPS relies on both the functionality of a machine millions of miles away in space and the intricacies of software. Sometimes, the GPS, much like a person reading a map, struggles to differentiate between a regular road and a remote trail. Additionally, GPS technology can also be compromised by inaccurate map data, leading individuals down paths that appear complete on GPS, only to end in a dead end.

There is a common misunderstanding about GPS, which is the belief that the military has a significant advantage over civilian GPS. Both military and civilian GPS systems utilize the same networks, satellites, and equipment. The only advantage that the military has is the use of two signals instead of one, which provides a backup in case one signal fails. However, even with two signals, military GPS has experienced failures. It is worth noting that the civilian network will also be transitioning to two signals in the near future.

Additional causes of GPS failure may include equipment malfunctions, software corruption, battery depletion, physical damage, and signal transmission issues. External factors such as weather conditions, obstacles like buildings, and interference from other electronic devices can also disrupt GPS signals. This is why phone usage is prohibited on flights, as it can interfere with the aircraft's GPS systems and other critical equipment.

It is not entirely accurate to believe that the government can track individuals through GPS devices like smartphones. While most GPS devices are receivers that only pick up signals from satellites and do not transmit signals, newer models of cell phones are now equipped to act as transceivers. However, this should not be confused with tracking phones through cell phone signals. Many apps and software, such as "find my phone," use cell signals from towers to determine a general location by triangulating the signal. This process involves sending a signal to the phone through the cell network and receiving a ping back from the nearest cell phone tower. While this can provide a general location, it does not pinpoint the exact location of the phone. Therefore, even though emergency dispatchers can ping a phone, it does not always guarantee that first responders can locate the individual. In urban areas with multiple towers, triangulating signals can provide a more accurate location, but in rural areas with fewer towers, the location may be several miles off.

CHAPTER NINE: DISASTERS

Chapter Nine: Disasters

Tornado

Tornadoes are characterized by violently rotating winds forming a funnel-shaped cloud and moving beneath a large storm system. Waterspouts are essentially tornadoes that develop over bodies of water, while multiple vortex tornadoes involve more than one vortex simultaneously. Tornadoes have the potential to form in any location worldwide and are usually seasonal, although they can happen at any point throughout the year.

Tornado Classifications

Weak	EFO, EF1	Winds speeds of 65 -110 mph
Strong	EF2, EF3	Winds speeds of 111 to 165 mph
Violent	EF4, EF5	Winds speeds of 166 to 200 mph or more

Source: U.S. National Weather Serve
Categories based on wind speed and damage potential.

Tornadoes are categorized according to the F-scale, a rating system created by Dr. Theodore Fujita. Originally, the F-scale numbers were determined by Dr. Fujita using the Beaufort wind scale, which measured wind speed in knots to assess damage. Although an updated version of the F-scale is now utilized, it is important to note that these classifications are still approximations and not entirely based on scientific evidence. The accurate measurement of tornado intensity remains a challenge, as the damage caused by tornadoes can differ significantly depending on the specific location.

EF#	# Second Gust (mph)
0	65 - 85
1	86 -110
2	111 - 135
3	136 - 165
4	166 - 200
5	Over 200
Estimating tornado strength based on F-scale developed by Dr Theodore Fujita	

Fallacy: You will hear a tornado before it strikes.

Tornadoes have the ability to hit unexpectedly and without any prior notice. In many cases, the noise from the wind and storm that accompany a tornado can mask the actual sound of the tornado itself. Tornadoes not only move swiftly, but they can also approach a person's vicinity before the individual even realizes the tornado's presence.

It is important for individuals to stay informed about the news and public service announcements regarding the possibility of tornadoes. While modern surveillance systems have become quite accurate in predicting when a tornado is likely to occur and tracking its path, they are still unable to accurately predict the exact location where a tornado will form. Therefore, it is crucial for people to take shelter when advised to do so, rather than waiting for the tornado to occur. The speed and destructive force of a tornado leave very little time or room for action once it is already active.

Lie: I can see the tornado coming.

Tornadoes often strike at night and during severe storms, which can significantly reduce visibility, particularly when driving. The combination of heavy rain, strong winds, and debris being thrown around can make it challenging to spot a tornado. The limited visibility and loud noise from the storm have caught many people off guard.

Myth: Tornados cannot cross mountain or hits cities.

It has been mentioned that tornadoes can manifest in any location worldwide and can traverse various types of terrain. Tornadoes can manifest within urban areas, suburban neighborhoods, and rural towns. It is important to note that tornadoes are not exclusive to trailer parks. The reason why trailer parks often suffer disproportionate damage is due to the construction and anchoring of trailers. The flimsy materials and weak structures of trailers make them susceptible to damage from even weaker tornadoes. Therefore, individuals residing in trailer parks should take precautions when the possibility of a tornado is high. The occurrence of a tornado is contingent upon the presence of specific weather conditions.

Lie: I only need to worry about tornado during "tornado season"

It has been mentioned that tornadoes require specific weather conditions to develop. They have the potential to form in any location and at any time. Although certain weather patterns typically occur during specific times of the year, leading to the concept of "tornado" or "hurricane" season, these natural disasters can still occur outside of their usual season.

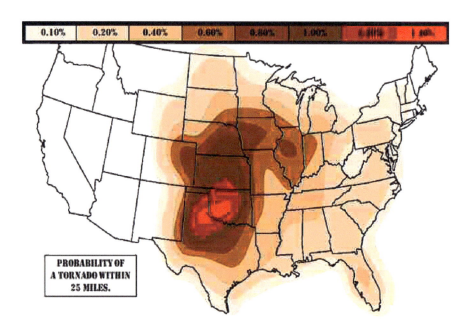

Myth: Open the window before the Tornado.

An ancient common belief suggests that a tornado outside could create a pressure disparity inside a closed residence, leading to windows shattering and causing harm and destruction inside the house. Research has shown that there is not a substantial pressure difference that would lead to windows or doors shattering within a home. The destruction of windows and other structures is usually due to severe wind speeds or debris. It is unnecessary to open windows or doors during a tornado. Similarly, the misconception that the same phenomenon occurs during severe storms has also been debunked.

Fallacy: you should seek safety under a bridge during a tornado.

The false notion that individuals are protected under an overpass during a tornado stems from a specific viral video depicting people taking cover under the overpass while a tornado passed above. Specialists suggest that the tornado in the video may have had minimal wind speed. Tornadoes of higher intensity have caused damage to overpass(s) and sturdier structures in the past. Seeking refuge under an overpass does not ensure safety. Stronger winds can penetrate under the overpass and scatter debris, potentially causing harm to individuals.

Fallacy: I only need to wait for the Siren.

There are two primary concerns when it comes to relying on tornado sirens. The first concern is that sirens are typically not activated until a tornado has already touched down or fully developed. The second concern is that in many areas, the decision to activate the sirens lies with a first responder who may be preoccupied with storm-related operations, causing delays in sounding the alarm. Additionally, specific criteria must be met before the siren can be activated, such as the operator needing to be in a particular location, which can further contribute to delays. Moreover, sirens are dependent on technology, which can fail due to various reasons, including the reliance on internet connectivity that many systems are transitioning to. The connectivity issues experienced in residential settings are often mirrored in organizational settings as well.

Trombes or Whirlwinds by
Camille Flammarion 1873

Earthquake:

An earthquake is a sudden and violent movement of the ground, often resulting in significant destruction, caused by shifts in the earth's crust or volcanic activity. It is also known as a tremor or quake. Earthquakes can displace or disrupt the ground, and when they occur at sea, they can displace enough seabed to cause a tsunami. While earthquakes typically happen in specific areas, the shockwaves from a severe quake can travel great distances. They often occur in a series, with many quakes that may or may not be felt and may or may not be severe or shallow. Aftershocks, smaller quakes that occur after a larger one, are common, so it is important to always be prepared for them. Sometimes, a large quake is mistaken as the main quake. In addition to the shaking of the quake, other disasters such as fires, tsunamis, floods, and landslides can also occur.

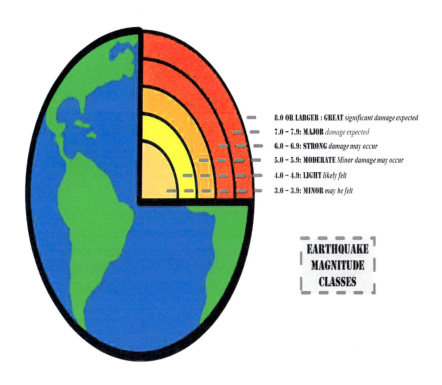

8.0 OR LARGER : GREAT *significant damage expected*

7.0 – 7.9: MAJOR *damage expected*

6.0 – 6.9: STRONG *damage may occur*

5.0 – 5.9: MODERATE *Minor damage may occur*

4.0 – 4.9: LIGHT *likely felt*

3.0 – 3.9: MINOR *may be felt*

EARTHQUAKE MAGNITUDE CLASSES

Myth: Triangle of life.

The triangle of life theory, perpetuated by a viral email linked to earthquakes, suggests that during an earthquake, individuals should position themselves next to a sturdy object such as a concrete pillar. This way, if objects begin to fall, they will lean against the solid structure, creating a void space between the leaning objects and the pillar. This void space is believed to be a safer area for the person to seek refuge.

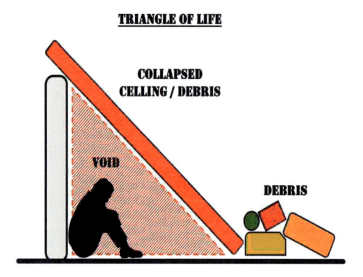

It is theoretically possible for one of these voids or triangles to occur during an earthquake, but it is impossible for an individual to predict where the point will be. Additionally, the speed at which an earthquake happens may prevent an individual from finding a safe position without risking injury. It is much safer to seek shelter under a sturdy object for protection rather than trying to move through a space during an earthquake.

Myth: Stand under doorways during an earthquake.

It may have been true in the past, but contemporary construction has shown that doorways are not necessarily safer than any other area of the house. It is advised to seek shelter under a robust table, ideally one with a sturdy build. Many modern pieces of furniture are made from subpar materials and may not withstand heavy loads, including the weight of a collapsing ceiling. The table remains the top choice as it can shield against smaller objects falling, like lamps or furniture tipping over. It is important to secure heavy furniture to the wall to prevent it from falling, earthquake or not.

Fallacy: You can always be airlifted.

Airlifting someone depends on various factors, including the availability of aircraft, landing zones, aircraft equipment, the situation at the scene, and the reason for the airlift. Weather conditions can often disrupt flights more than anticipated. Factors such as danger, harsh terrain, and obstructions at the scene can also pose challenges for landing and takeoff. Additionally, distance plays a role as it can take time to reach the individual or transport them to a facility. In some areas, there may only be one available aircraft, which can lead to issues if it is already in use. Finally, maintenance and fuel issues with the vehicle itself can also result in problems.

Fallacy: The shelters are safe.

In the event of a disaster, individuals may find themselves alone for a portion or the entirety of the crisis. It is crucial to understand that if a disaster is severe enough to necessitate sheltering in place, first responders will be occupied elsewhere. Consequently, those seeking refuge in shelters may need to fend for themselves against potential threats. Conditions within shelters can escalate from minor annoyances among people to theft, robbery, and even more serious offenses. For instance, during hurricane Katrina, the majority of violent incidents took place within the shelters designed to provide safety, rather than out in the city.

Lie: You should tape your windows before a storm.

Taping windows before a storm may seem like a sensible idea, but it is ultimately ineffective and could pose a greater risk. There is no guarantee that taping will protect the window from storm debris or strong winds. In fact, taping the glass could result in larger and more hazardous pieces of glass if the window breaks. This false sense of security could lead homeowners to leave thinking their home is secure, only to return and find it exposed to the elements. Instead of taping, it is more practical to board up the window or invest in stormproof shutters.

The use of tape on windows has proven to be ineffective in preventing flooding, as water pressure can cause the entire glass pane to break through the frame, or water may seep in through gaps in the window or other areas of the building.

Lie: Wind during a hurricane kill more than the water.

Wind is a potential danger during hurricanes and tropical storms, but statistics indicate that the greatest danger actually comes from surge flooding. While many focus on protecting themselves and their homes from wind and rain damage, they often overlook the risks of rising water, flooding, and tidal waves. Hurricanes can cause a surge of flooding by pushing large amounts of water onshore, particularly in areas that are not typically affected, catching many off guard. A 50-year study highlighted that rainfall flooding resulted in more deaths during hurricanes and tropical storms than any other factor, including tornado-induced winds.

2021 Weather Fatalities

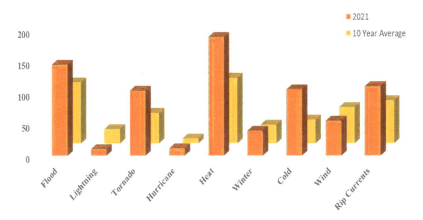

Hurricane/Tropical Cyclone fatalities, injuries, & damage are attributed to wind. other damage, injuries, and fatalities are listed within their separate event types.

Data collected from the U.S. National Weather Service.

Fallacy: I will not need my documents because they are online.

It is essential to scan and store important documents on a thumb drive for easy access while traveling. Credit cards, passports, and social security cards should be kept in a readily accessible container to grab quickly before leaving. Countless individuals have experienced the shock of returning home after a short trip, only to find their residence gone or their documents ruined.

It is advisable to keep important documents on hand, as the process of obtaining new ones can be extremely challenging due to bureaucratic hurdles. Many government systems require specific forms of identification to obtain another form of identification, and providing just one piece of proof can result in months or even years of paperwork to verify a person's identity. Some systems can create a never-ending cycle, such as requiring a photo ID to obtain a social security card, and vice versa. At the very least, individuals should carry a photo ID (such as a driver's license, passport, or immigration card), their social security card, and their birth certificate to start over if necessary.

Individuals with medical conditions, particularly those necessitating specific medications such as narcotics, must also guarantee that they possess the correct medical documentation, or else they may be forced to forgo their medication or undergo the entire medical procedure once more.

| HOUSEHOLD IDENTIFICATION | Think about the documents you would need to identify yourself and your household members, including children and pets, your relationships, or status. These may include: |

☐ Vital records (birth, marriage, divorce certificate, adoption, child custody papers)

☐ Passport, driver's license, Social Security Card, green card, military service identification, other

☐ Pet ownership papers, identification tags

MEDICAL IDENTIFICATION

Partial document list from FEMA

☐ Health/dental insurance, Medicare, Medicaid, VA health benefits

☐ List of medications, immunizations, allergies, prescriptions, medical equipment and devices, pharmacy information

☐ Living will, medical power of attorney

☐ Caregiver agency contract or service agreement

☐ Disabilities documentation

☐ Contact information for doctors / specialists, dentists, pediatricians, veterinarians

Lie: use the dishwasher as a safe.

One specific unconventional thinker reasoned that a dishwasher designed to fill up with water and prevent leaking when washing dishes would be perfectly designed to be sealed preventing water entering from the outside. This led to the false belief that the dishwasher seal would protect valuables and important documents from outside flooding, advocating for them to be placed inside the dishwasher for safekeeping. However, the truth is that a dishwasher's seal can easily be broken during a disaster. Most dishwashers only maintain a seal while the machine is in operation, and others can easily have the seal disrupted.

Important documents should be taken with the individual when possible. There are relatively cheap watertight containers being sold that do a far better job at security and protecting the items. An alternative use for the dishwasher would be to fill it up with as much ice as possible during a power outage and place perishable food inside. The ice will help preserve the food, and when it melts, it travels down the dishwasher drain, and even a flimsy seal on the dishwasher will help hold in the cold for a while.

Lie: Jump before the elevator hits the ground.

It is scientifically impossible to survive a falling elevator by jumping just before it hits the ground, regardless of the speed and height of the fall. A recommended but unproven method is to lie flat on the elevator floor to distribute the impact damage.

Fortunately, there are multiple safety features installed in elevators to prevent them from falling, especially in the U.S. and in newer models. The annual rate of deaths due to falling elevators is less than 1%. Injuries typically occur because of other elevator malfunctions, such as doors closing on someone's appendages. Interestingly, the number of injuries from falling down the stairs still exceeds the injuries caused by elevators.

Avalanche:

Avalanches are a swift movement of snow down a slope, typically a mountainside or hill, that can cause damage and injury as it moves. They are mainly made up of trapped air and snow, but can also contain ice, rocks, trees, and other debris as they travel. There are two kinds of avalanches: slab avalanches, which are made up of tightly packed snow triggered by the collapse of a weak underlying snow layer, and loose snow avalanches, which consist of looser snow. Avalanches gain speed and size quickly as they gather more snow. They are more common in spring and winter but can happen at any time of the year. An avalanche can occur on any mountainside or large hill with significant amounts of snow.

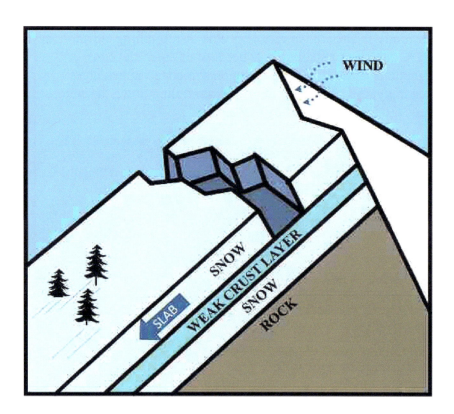

Fallacy: If buried during an avalanche spit to find direction.

Being trapped under an avalanche can lead to disorientation, with individuals finding themselves buried in various directions due to a combination of pressure, injuries, and suffocation. When attempting to dig their way out, it is important to remember that visibility is severely limited when buried under ice, making it difficult to determine which way is up. Additionally, there may not be enough space to even spit or see the direction in which the spit falls.

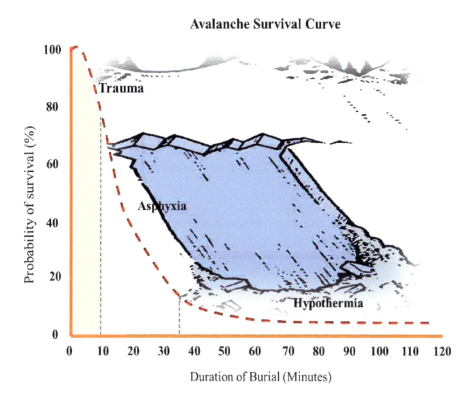

Avalanche Survival Curve

Myth: Lighting does not strike the same place twice.

Lightning can indeed strike the same spot more than once, despite the popular myth. Tall, isolated objects, particularly those made of metal, are especially attractive to lightning. In major cities, many buildings are struck anywhere from twenty-five to one hundred times a year.

Myth: Crouching down will protect you from lighting.

Tall objects attract lightning, leading to the misconception that smaller ones are safer. However, there is no evidence to support the idea that crouching down will protect from a lightning strike. The safest place during a lightning storm is a building grounded from electrical strikes, while structures such as sheds, porches, awnings, and gazebos are not safe.

Myth: crouching on a sleeping pad will insulate from a lightning strike.

Crouching down on a rubber or plastic sleeping mat during a lightning strike is believed to insulate oneself from the ground electrical current, but commercial mats are not designed to protect against the voltage of a lightning strike. Grounding mats specifically designed for electrical work can help prevent electrical shock, but they are not intended for outdoor activities or lightning strikes. It is uncertain whether these mats would be effective in preventing a lightning strike during a storm, and carrying one around during adventures would be impractical.

Fallacy: You must wait for the car to fill up with water before escaping when submerged.

It is a widespread misconception that a person trapped inside a submerged car must wait for the vehicle to be completely underwater before attempting to open the door, as the pressure outside the car is believed to be greater than inside. While this concept is scientifically accurate, the reality is that the individual may risk drowning or not be able to hold their breath long enough for the car to equalize pressure. This scenario is often sensationalized in the media for dramatic effect, but it is not a practical approach in real-life situations.

The best approach is to wait until the car is submerged in water up to chest level, then take a deep breath, hold your nose, pull the door handle, and push as forcefully as you can to hopefully open the door. Another option is to remove the headrest in most modern vehicles and use the metal prongs to break the glass on the door, allowing for escape through the window.

Lie: Hiding in cave or depression during wildfire.

An incorrect belief often circulated about wildfires is the notion that individuals can survive by seeking refuge in a depression or cave until the fire subsides. However, the lack of oxygen in such enclosed spaces can lead to suffocation before the fire dissipates. It is more advisable for individuals to attempt to escape by moving through the front of the flames, ensuring to shield as much skin as possible and safeguarding the eyes, mouth, nose, and face. Additionally, seeking an area with minimal vegetation can increase the chances of survival as the fire intensity is likely to be lower in such locations.

Fallacy: I can trust the weather forecast.

Weather forecasting is a highly complex discipline, which is why advanced education in this field typically requires a doctoral degree. It encompasses various sciences, mathematics, and human observation. Our understanding of the intricate workings of the world, including how different processes interact, remains limited. Mistakes in weather prediction often stem from this lack of comprehension, as well as from the limitations of the tools used to gather data. Technological shortcomings can lead to slow, flawed, or incomplete information. Despite these challenges, significant progress has been made in weather prediction. Currently, forecasts can accurately predict the weather up to seven days in advance with an 80% success rate, and up to five days in advance with a 90% success rate.

Lie: covering a nuclear blast with thumb means you're out of harm's way.

It has been suggested that extending one's arm, sticking out the thumb, and covering the nuclear blast with the thumb can protect a person from nuclear fallout. This notion may have gained popularity through the video game industry, but it has been proven to be baseless. A study proposed that an individual might be shielded from a significant amount of radiation using this method, but not entirely. The study also concluded that the person must be positioned upwind of the blast and moving away from it to ensure safety. While there is a slight chance that the thumb technique could be effective, experts advise that anyone who can see the blast should evacuate as
far and as quickly (preferably upwind) from the blast as possible.

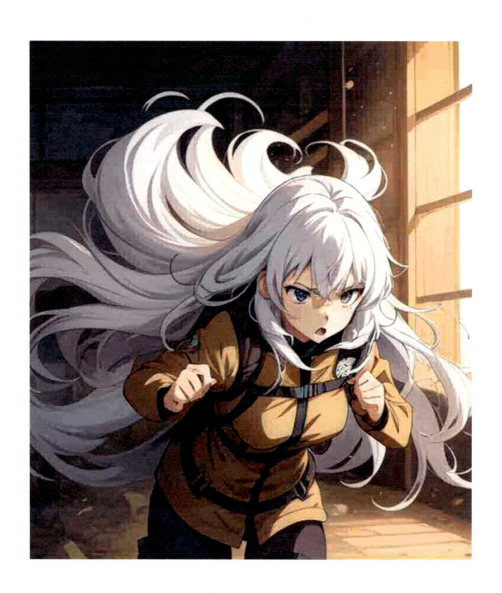

CHAPTER TEN: SELF-DEFENSE

Chapter Ten: Self-Defense

Fallacy: In firearms stopping power is the most important:

The notion of stopping power is inherently tied to the bullet caliber employed in a firearm. Generally speaking, a larger caliber results in a more pronounced impact, or stopping power, when the firearm is discharged. In the context of firearms for personal protection and self-defense, the primary considerations are the shooter's skill level and their comfort with the weapon.

The importance of stopping power is paramount when evaluating situations that involve body armor, long-range shooting, and the specific type of game targeted. Sufficient stopping power is essential for survival, particularly in encounters with large animals such as bears and during big game hunting. Ammunition ranging from 9mm to 7.62 caliber is adaptable and effective across a variety of scenarios. Calibers below 9mm are better suited for small game hunting and are less effective for self-defense applications. Conversely, calibers exceeding 7.62 are generally reserved for sniping, combat, and big game hunting, making them less practical for survival situations. Additionally, stopping power is affected by factors like bullet weight (measured in grains) and velocity (measured in feet per second), with their impact varying according to the caliber of the ammunition.

Size	Grains	Bullet Diameter	Muzzle Velocity (FPS)	Muzzle Energy (Ft.ibs)
.22	40	0.69	1255	140
.380	85	1.12	1000	189
.357	158	1.12	1235	535
9mm	115	1.12	1225	383
10mm	155	1.26	1386	660
.40	180	1.26	950	360
.45	230	1.41	830	345
.223	55	0.70	3240	1282
7.62mm	125	0.94	2400	1600
12GA	438	2.29	1600	2490

Fallacy: Books, Magazines, and Newspaper can be used as a bullet proof vest.

The belief that a large collection of magazines, newspapers, and books can function as a makeshift bulletproof vest is a fallacy. The primary concern is the extensive amount of material required to effectively stop a bullet. A considerable volume of these items would be necessary to provide adequate protection, rendering it impractical to quickly gather and secure them in vital areas of the body. Additionally, the vest's effectiveness in stopping a bullet is dependent on the distance from which the shot is fired, the closer the shooter, the greater the bullet's penetration. Other factors, such as the caliber of the bullet, the efficiency of the firearm, and the bullet's stopping power, also play a significant role in determining effectiveness.

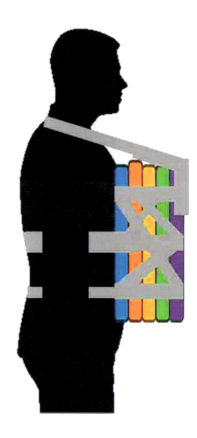

Fallacy: Chloroform instantly knocking you out.

Chloroform is a colorless, odorless substance with a sweet aroma that was utilized as a general anesthetic and sedative from the 19th century until the mid-20th century. Its use as a sedative has contributed to its depiction in movies as a knockout agent. Many viewers recognize scenes where a suspicious character covers a victim's mouth and nose with a cloth, resulting in immediate unconsciousness. Chloroform has been exploited in various criminal acts. Infamously, serial killer H. H. Holmes used chloroform to overdose his victims, and there have been cases of sexual offenders using it to incapacitate their victims. The key difference between fiction and reality is the time it takes for chloroform to induce unconsciousness, which can be as long as five minutes. This delay often drives criminals to opt for other methods or to target individuals who are smaller or weaker, making them less able to resist.

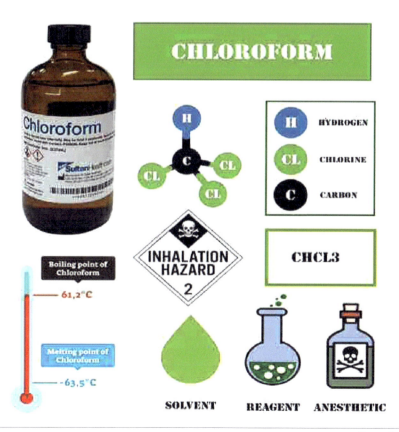

"The Dwarf's Chamber" Engraving from The British Library

Fallacy: Stun guns knock you out.

A prominent theme in film involves the use of stun guns to render individuals incapacitated. It is crucial to differentiate between a taser and a stun gun, despite their similar operational principles. A stun gun requires direct contact with a person to function effectively, whereas a taser discharges two prongs that transmit an electrical current to a target from a distance. The underlying mechanics of these devices are complex, but fundamentally, the electrical current interacts with the body's own electrical signals, resulting in involuntary muscle contractions. This reaction leads to temporary paralysis and drains the muscles' energy, thereby weakening the target. Tasers are preferred because they affect both sensory and motor nerves, while stun guns mainly induce pain and may only impact a specific area of the body. In contrast, tasers influence the entire body, causing pain and immobilizing all muscles. However, their effectiveness is not guaranteed, as individuals with high pain thresholds, those under the influence of certain substances, or individuals with mental health challenges may resist the effects of the electrical shock.

In conversations regarding self-defense devices, shock sticks and cattle prods often appear alongside stun guns as viable alternatives. These tools are designed to deliver a low voltage that inflicts a mild level of pain. They do not generate enough current to interfere with muscle function, enabling individuals with moderate to high pain tolerance to persist in a confrontation despite the shock. Occasionally, military personnel train with stun knives that offer a comparable shock experience, mimicking the sensation of being cut or stabbed, to enhance their ability to cope with injuries in combat situations.

Individuals must exercise caution regarding the misunderstandings associated with high-voltage devices. Claims suggesting that a device can generate over 3 million volts are deceptive, as small devices with restricted power capabilities cannot reach such voltage levels. It is crucial to recognize that voltage and power are not synonymous.

Myth: just carry pepper spray.

Pepper spray functions as a potent irritant that operates on the principle of pain compliance to achieve its intended effect. To maximize its efficacy, the spray needs to hit the soft tissues of the body, especially the eyes. In high-pressure scenarios, particularly for untrained users, accurately aiming at an assailant can prove difficult. There is also the potential risk of accidentally spraying oneself. Various factors, including lack of familiarity with the device, strong winds, and heightened emotions, can contribute to unintentional self-spraying rather than effectively targeting an aggressor.

A significant issue with depending exclusively on pepper spray and stun guns for self-defense is their reliance on pain compliance. People have different pain thresholds, and many offenders may have a greater tolerance than the general population. Law enforcement personnel are subjected to pepper spray during their training to comprehend the discomfort faced by suspects and to develop the ability to operate effectively despite the pain. If police officers can adapt to the effects of pepper spray, it is reasonable to assume that criminals can as well.

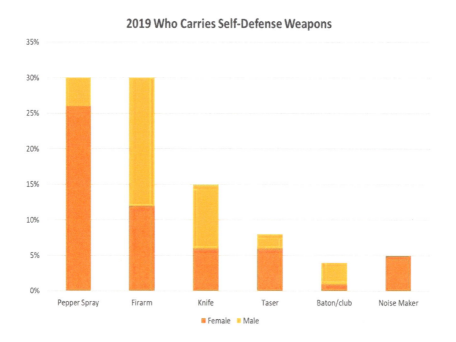

Fallacy: I'll get a dog.

Dogs can serve as excellent self-defense and security measures; however, their effectiveness is accompanied by several caveats. While many individuals view dogs as integral members of their families, it is essential to remember that they are still animals. Their reliability in critical situations can sometimes be uncertain. An animal's instincts, behaviors, and emotional states can be influenced by malicious individuals. For instance, a burglar might distract a security dog with food, allowing them to bypass the animal while it is preoccupied. There are centuries old document explaining techniques to bypass military and security dogs; these techniques still work today.

Another important consideration is training. Many individuals acquire a dog with the expectation that it will instinctively provide protection. However, a dog's protective instincts are influenced by several factors, with breed being the most significant. Certain breeds are known to be highly protective of specific family members or the family unit, while others may show little concern for the presence of strangers.

Additionally, a dog's upbringing and the way it is nurtured by its owners play a crucial role in its behavior. Some dogs may exhibit overprotectiveness as they age or when they are unwell, while others may become less protective. This variability underscores the importance of proper training tailored to the intended purpose of the dog. If a dog is needed for self-defense, it is essential to have it specifically trained for that role.

Environmental factors can also impact a dog's behavior; for instance, a protection dog that spends excessive time engaging in play with the family may become more docile and less inclined to defend. Police and military dogs must adhere to strict discipline and training regimens throughout their careers to ensure they respond appropriately to commands when needed. Many law enforcement officers have encountered challenges with their dogs' following commands when they have been trained more as pets than as disciplined protection resources.

Another consideration is the dependence on the owner to effectively manage the dog. Many owners become complacent in their training efforts and often overlook the proper commands needed to achieve desired behaviors from their dogs. Additionally, owners may not always have their dogs with them, when necessary, as they might be unable to take their pets to certain locations where risks are present. There are instances when the dog is at the veterinarian, in a kennel, or in a shelter. Predators may take advantage of these situations, waiting for the owner to secure the dog in their vehicle before launching an attack.

"Fleeing" by Thomas Lord Busby 1826, Etching

Fallacy: I'll just carry a gun.

Firearms serve as effective self-defense tools; however, they come with significant restrictions. Law-abiding citizens face limitations regarding when and where they can carry a firearm. Locations such as schools, hospitals, and airports prohibit firearms in their vicinity. Additionally, specialized training is essential not only for the effective use of a firearm but also for understanding the appropriate circumstances for its use. Those who express discomfort with firearms in their presence may not fully grasp the realities of crowded situations, where drawing a firearm can be challenging. In densely populated areas, the use of a firearm can pose serious risks. Regular practice is necessary to handle a firearm competently in various scenarios. Furthermore, the cultural context of a region can complicate the act of carrying a firearm, making it burdensome. For instance, openly carrying a pistol in a holster is common in the southern United States, but attempting the same in major urban areas may lead to law enforcement intervention.

Fallacy: Car doors as bullet proof.

The media has once again contributed to the public's erroneous belief that car doors provide a safe barrier against gunfire. Bullets can penetrate car doors with ease. Numerous police shooting incidents have demonstrated the fallacy of this assumption. Modern car doors are constructed from thin layers of metal, plastic, and Styrofoam, making them vulnerable to bullet penetration.

Myth: silencers are silent.

The portrayal of firearms in movies and television often deviates significantly from reality. While media aims to entertain, it frequently overlooks important aspects of firearms to advance the narrative, resulting in a disregard for the complexities involved. A prime example of this misunderstanding is the depiction of silencer effectiveness, which is often exaggerated in terms of noise reduction.

A silencer, also known as a suppressor, regulates the volume of gas expelled from a firearm at the muzzle. This gas is accompanied by the sound wave generated by the bullet's propellant. Typically, the sound of a gunshot is quite loud and can be heard from several miles away in certain situations. The silencer features multiple baffles within the device, allowing the bullet to pass while redirecting the expelled gases along a longer route. This alteration in gas flow diminishes the sound of the gunshot, reduces the accompanying flash, and lessens the recoil. Research indicates that silencers can lower the sound of a gunshot by approximately 17 to 32 dB, which still renders them audible. For context, a reduction of 17-32 dB is comparable to a soft whisper. It is important to note that this measurement represents the upper range, as most silencers typically operate between 102 and 120 db.

A common misconception regarding silencers is that they eliminate the need for hearing protection. Although it is accurate that the noise produced by a silencer is less disruptive, enabling users to concentrate better and remain aware of their surroundings, the sound levels can still be loud enough to cause hearing damage. Extended exposure to sounds at or above 85 dB can result in hearing loss for many individuals.

Myth: Fake cameras for security.

Most decoy security cameras can be easily identified by criminals, including amateur ones. Nowadays, there are numerous affordable security camera options available, making it much simpler to implement genuine security measures rather than relying on the false sense of security that decoys provide to save money.

Fallacy: Keys as a weapon.

An outdated self-defense technique for women suggests placing a key between the fingers and using a fist to strike an assailant. However, this method has significant drawbacks. Many individuals do not have keychains that facilitate a quick setup, and there is a heightened risk of injuring oneself during the strike.

Fallacy: use of lasers.

Lasers mounted on weapons are often perceived as impressive, yet they are frequently misunderstood. Many people assume that a laser guarantees accuracy when firing. However, the precision of a shot is primarily determined by the shooter's skill and the correct alignment of the firearm, regardless of whether a laser or optical sight is used. If the weapon is not properly calibrated, even a laser that appears to be aimed directly at the target can result in a miss. Additionally, a shooter's technique, including grip, breathing, and stance, plays a crucial role; without proper fundamentals, the bullet may still stray off course. Furthermore, the type of laser can create a misleading impression, as some lasers can project further and more effectively than the weapon or ammunition can achieve.

Fallacy: Blade on Blade.

Films often portray sword and knife fights as far more exhilarating than they are. When two blades collide with significant force, the quality of the metal can lead to chipping, bending, or even breaking. This is why martial arts training typically emphasizes techniques such as parrying or evading during combat. In instances where contact is intentional, fighters frequently use the flat side of the blade to deflect attacks, or they rely on specific sections of the weapon that are thicker and reinforced to withstand impacts. A prominent illustration of this misconception can be found in samurai films that often show blade on blade combat with the traditional blades colliding so that the actors can get face to face to speak. The Samurai rarely engages in direct blade-to-blade contact, as such encounters would quickly damage the sword.

Myth: This Martial art vs. That Martial art.

No single martial art can be deemed superior to another. The key determinant of effectiveness lies in an individual's practice and discipline. A person who has dedicated years to mastering one particular art may demonstrate greater effectiveness in a confrontation, even when facing an opponent who employs a technically superior style or technique.

Many martial arts, despite their rigorous training, exhibit significant limitations in certain aspects. For instance, boxing may prove ineffective when faced with a skilled grappler. While self-defense specialists often debate the superiority of one art over another, there is a consensus that a well-rounded fighter must incorporate various disciplines to effectively defend against a range of situations.

To develop well-rounded individuals, it is essential to incorporate techniques in striking, grappling, blocking, throwing, joint manipulation, weapon usage, evasion, distance management, and transitions.

Most Popular Martial Arts for Self-Defense
Muay Thai
Krav Maga
Jiu-Jitsu (Brazilian)
Mixed Martial Arts (MMA)
Wrestling
Judo
Sambo
Karate
Taekwondo
Wing Chun
Aikido
Jeet Kune Do
Savate
Silat
Boxing
Reality-Based Self Defense (RBSD)/ Combatives

CHAPTER ELEVEN: MISCELLANEOUS

Chapter Eleven: Miscellaneous

Myth: Cost equals quality.

Big corporations often promote the notion that higher prices equate to better quality to increase their profits. While it is true that quality products generally come with a higher price tag, not all expensive items are necessarily of superior quality. Fashion is a prime example of how the perceived value of an item is often based on the brand name rather than the actual quality of the product.

It is an unfortunate reality that only a small number of products worldwide are crafted with a focus on quality. Most items are manufactured with cost-efficiency as the primary goal. One rationale behind prioritizing cost over quality is that durable products are less frequently replaced, which could negatively affect sales for businesses that rely on repeat purchases.

This misconception is further supported by the fact that most products are manufactured by a small number of factories worldwide, yet they are sold under different brand names at varying prices. For instance, Hanes T-shirts and Kanye West Brand Shirts are produced in the same factory but are priced significantly different. Similarly, all mattresses are manufactured in just four factories globally, but they are labeled with different brand names depending on the location of sale.

Warning: Consumers must exercise caution when making purchases, as numerous companies produce counterfeit products that closely resemble the genuine items at a lower price. A notable instance is the surge of counterfeit C.A.T. tourniquets during the Iraq/Afghanistan war. These items were significantly cheaper than the authentic ones, but they were poorly constructed and ultimately ineffective in combat situations, potentially leading to loss of life.

Caution: Consumers should also stay informed about updates regarding reputable businesses, especially if there are any modifications in the production process. Several consumers who have placed their trust in companies for an extended period have faced significant challenges or financial losses by relying on a company's product, only to discover that the company has relocated its manufacturing operations to a new facility that produces inferior products.

Fallacy: Military Grade

The concept of military grade is intended to link a product with the overall image of the military; one that is tough, reliable, and long-lasting, much like the members of our armed forces. Unfortunately, the term military grade is simply a marketing ploy that companies use to persuade consumers that the product is of higher quality than it truly is. It is similar to the tactics of "sex sells" or "my favorite celebrity uses it."

Military-grade products are expected to elicit a response of increased durability and sustainability. If a product can withstand the harsh conditions of the military, it should perform well for civilian use. True military equipment, vehicles, and supplies are typically built by the lowest bidder. This means that the individual who offers the military the lowest price gets to supply the product. However, the cheapest option is not always the best in terms of quality. While not all military items are subpar, there are some exceptional products that are highly effective for their intended purposes. Interestingly, these items are often not labeled as military-grade.

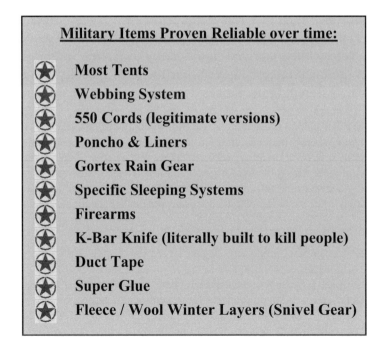

Military Items Proven Reliable over time:

- Most Tents
- Webbing System
- 550 Cords (legitimate versions)
- Poncho & Liners
- Gortex Rain Gear
- Specific Sleeping Systems
- Firearms
- K-Bar Knife (literally built to kill people)
- Duct Tape
- Super Glue
- Fleece / Wool Winter Layers (Snivel Gear)

The U.S. government once implemented a military grading system for certain products to guarantee that the quality of items purchased by the government meets specific standards. Substandard products could potentially lead to loss of life or significant financial burden on the government. However, with shifts in military policies and politics, the concept of military grading is now obsolete, except for a few select items. The majority of these items are not utilized by the general public.

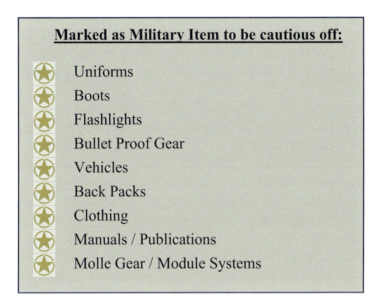

Marked as Military Item to be cautious off:

- Uniforms
- Boots
- Flashlights
- Bullet Proof Gear
- Vehicles
- Back Packs
- Clothing
- Manuals / Publications
- Molle Gear / Module Systems

Note: Military publications should be cross referenced with other sources to ensure their viability. Many publications are outdated. Other military items should be reviewed from various sources before purchasing. Some items have better civilian equivalents out there and other items have so many counterfeit equivalents that it is hard to find a quality product.

Lie: All knives are created equal

The notion that all knives are the same or that any knife will suffice is a result of ignorance or sheer foolishness. Those who regularly use knives can attest to the fact that not every knife is suitable for every task. Extensive literature exists solely on the topic of selecting the right knife. The variety of knives available varies depending on factors such as environment, culture, intended purpose, materials at hand, and local regulations. A knife designed for self-defense may not be practical for survival, and vice versa.

Several general recommendations for survival knives include the necessity of being full tang. Full tang knives are known for their durability during tough tasks, and even if the handle breaks, the knife can still be used. Avoid using double-bladed knives, as single-edged blades are more suitable for self-defense and combat. A survival knife should have one flat edge for techniques like "batoning". Serrated edges have their pros and cons - when located on the non-edge side, they can hinder certain techniques like "batoning", but they are useful for sawing branches and can still be effective when dull. Plain edges are better for precise cuts, as serrated edges may interfere with the cut if located on the blade side.

Carrying a survival knife is often misunderstood. It is advisable for individuals to have two different types of knives: a larger one for tasks in the wilderness and a smaller one for intricate issues.

Batoning: the technique of splitting or cutting wood using a baton – sized stick or mallet to repeatedly strike the spine of a sturdy knife, chisel, or blade to drive it through wood. Used to make kindling or desired forms such a boards, slats, or notches.

Consideration when Choosing a Knife

1. Strong and Versatile.
2. Can hunt and clean pray.
3. Can fend off predators.
4. Help with woodwork and starting a fire.
5. Does not rust easily.
6. Can be sharpened in the wild.

Fallacy: I can just make biodiesel, or biodiesel is easy to make.

Creating biodiesel may seem simple at first, but the process depends on the availability of supplies. Specialized equipment and knowledge are required, and obtaining oil, lye, and alcohol can be challenging, especially during a disaster. While lye and oil can be made at home, the process is time-consuming and requires specific materials. The appendices provide guides on making these components, giving individuals an idea of the complexity of biodiesel production without easy access to supplies.

Fallacy: There will be plenty of (useful) trash lying around.

It is an unfortunate reality that trash can be found almost everywhere on Earth, no matter where one travels. While some may argue that discarded items could potentially be repurposed for survival, the likelihood of finding truly useful trash is quite slim. Even if one does come across something like a water bottle, it may be damaged or unusable. Therefore, the idea of relying on finding useful trash for survival is not a reliable strategy and requires a great deal of resourcefulness and creativity.

Myth: You must wait 24-48 hours to report someone missing.

The idea that a person needs to wait 24-48 hours before reporting someone missing is a misconception popularized by movies and TV shows. The media tends to depict the military and law enforcement as less capable than they truly are, as without this portrayal, the storyline would not hold up. Reporting a missing person as soon as possible makes it easier for law enforcement to initiate a search. The urgency of the situation varies based on the individual circumstances, evidence, and context of the disappearance. All law enforcement agencies in the United States will act promptly upon receiving a report.

The AMBER Alert system was established in memory of 9-year-old Amber Hagerman, who was abducted and tragically killed while riding her bike in Arlington, Texas in 1996. This alert is utilized to seek assistance from the public in finding children who are in danger. The acronym "AMBER" represents "America's Missing Broadcast Emergency Response."

During the 1980s, images of missing children were commonly featured on milk cartons, a practice that persisted until the 1990s. Regrettably, this portrayal has since been trivialized in the media. The utilization of milk carton advertisements was eventually replaced by the AMBER alert system.

AMBER: issued when a child is believed to have been abducted may be in danger of assault, bodily injury or death

SILVER: issued for missing older adults who suffer from an impaired mental condition such as Alzheimer's or dementia

BLUE: issued for wanted person who are suspected of killing a seriously injuring a law enforcement officer.

ENDANGERED MISSING: issued for missing person with an intellectual disability or developmental disorder.

CAMO: issued for missing current or former members of the military who suffer from a documented mental illness

CLEAR: issued for missing adults who may be in imminent danger of injury or death, or whose disappearance is believed to be involuntary.

MISSING

FULL NAME

Date of Birth:

Age:

Sex or gender:

Race:

Eyes:

Hair:

Height:

Weight:

Wearing:

Identifying Characteristics:

CLEAR PHOTO

LAST SEEN: MONTH, DAY, YEAR

IF YOU HAVE ANY INFORMATION ABOUT (NAME) PLEASE CONTACT:

Lie: You do not need writing material in survival gear, bug-out-bag, etc...

Numerous factors must be considered when it comes to ensuring survival, with one of these factors being the weight that an individual may need to carry. The military emphasizes the importance of every ounce, as no one desires to traverse long distances across challenging landscapes burdened by unnecessary weight. As a result, certain individuals, whether considered experts or not, may argue that carrying writing equipment is superfluous.

There are numerous compelling reasons to carry writing tools, such as a small notebook and pen or pencil. When faced with survival situations, individuals may experience dehydration, exposure, hunger, stress, anxiety, and other mental challenges. Some of these conditions can lead to memory and focus issues. Writing materials can assist in keeping track of crucial information to help the survivalist stay focused on staying alive, such as marking food sources, mapping the surroundings, noting areas already explored, and more. Additionally, writing tools can serve as a source of comfort by providing a distraction or peace of mind. Jotting down thoughts can alleviate boredom during survival tasks. While it may seem grim, having writing materials allows for the recording of final thoughts and wishes. For instance, wildlife photographer Carl McCunn, who became stranded in Alaska and ran out of supplies, was able to convey his last wishes and reasons for suicide before taking his own life. Authorities were able to piece together the fate of the renowned Christopher McCandless from the film/book "Into the Wild" thanks to the journal he left behind.

Fallacy: I can just build it.

The die-hard proponents (or impostors) will always argue for the lack of tools in certain situations by claiming that a person can simply create one. For instance, crafting a spear for fishing or hunting, or fashioning a knife from stone. Although humans have been crafting efficient tools for survival tasks for millennia, much of this knowledge has been lost over time. Those who excel in toolmaking are typically specialists in a particular type of tool; for example, one survival expert may excel at crafting blades from minerals (flint knapping), while another may be skilled at making primitive bows. Rarely does one individual possess expertise in all types of tools. Even among ancient societies and primitive tribes today, there is usually a designated expert for each specific tool's construction. It is important to approach with caution the methods employed by these so-called experts, as they often rely on modern items or techniques to create these primitive tools. An individual should dedicate countless hours to mastering the art of toolmaking in a safe environment before depending on their ability to replicate results in a survival scenario with limited energy, time, and resources.

Fallacy: Plenty of gas lying around.

Apocalyptic films often showcase the abundance of gasoline or petrol, suggesting that it could be a valuable resource in a post-apocalyptic world. However, while it is true that some gasoline may still be accessible for survival purposes, there are numerous challenges and drawbacks associated with depending on its availability.

Gasoline typically remains viable for only about three to six months, regardless of the storage method used. Over time, the gasoline will begin to evaporate, resulting in a decrease in availability. The remaining gasoline will also lose its effectiveness due to oxidation, a chemical process where the compound either loses an electron or gains oxygen. Essentially, the longer gasoline is stored, the more its chemical composition changes. On the other hand, diesel fuel can last longer, ranging from six to twelve months, especially when stored in a cool environment at approximately 70°F and treated with biocides and stabilizers.

Another common misconception is the practice of siphoning gas. This involves inserting a tube into the gas tank and using suction to draw the gas out. The process relies on the principle that the gas tank is positioned higher than the container, allowing gravity to assist in transferring the gas. However, siphoning gas using the mouth-to-tube technique can be challenging and potentially dangerous, as it may result in inhaling gas fumes. Moreover, most modern vehicles are equipped with anti-siphoning mechanisms, making this method ineffective. An alternative approach is to drain the fuel line, although this requires specific tools and knowledge of the vehicle's construction. Specialized siphoning devices with a suction bulb are available at auto parts stores to avoid using the mouth-to-hose method. Nevertheless, these devices do not address the issue of anti-siphoning devices, which can be bypassed with specialized expertise and tools.

Obtaining gas from gas stations during disasters presents two significant challenges. Firstly, most pumps rely on electricity to function, meaning that the gas station must have power in order to access the gas. Additionally, attempting to extract gas directly from the tank faces similar obstacles to siphoning gas in a car, as anti-siphoning technology prevents unauthorized access without specialized equipment and expertise. While there are a few older stations where gas can be easily retrieved by opening the hatch, these are quite rare and typically located in remote rural areas. Moreover, there are additional hurdles such as bypassing hatch locks and needing a specific tool to open certain hatches.

Fallacy: Telling time by using the sun (finger method).

One practical way to estimate the time remaining until sunset is by using an individual's fingers, the horizon, and the sun. To apply this technique, a person should face the sun with a clear view of the horizon. They should then raise their hand in the air, aligning the bottom edge of their hand with the sun's diameter and the other edge of their hand towards the horizon. The person will then count the number of fingers it takes to reach the horizon, with each finger representing fifteen minutes. For instance, if it takes six fingers, then six times fifteen would equal 90 minutes (15x6=90) or one hour and thirty minutes. Each hand signifies one hour (15 minutes x 4 fingers = 60 minutes or 1 hour), so each hand it takes to reach the horizon represents an hour. For example, if it takes three hand lengths to reach the horizon, then it is three hours until sunset. By knowing the time of sunset, an individual can subtract the counted time from the sunset time to estimate the current time. This method is most effective towards the end of the day. Those who are familiar with the outdoors can use the assumption that the sun directly overhead is noon and this technique to gauge how much daylight remains.

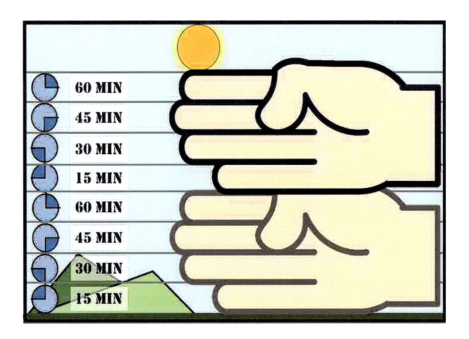

To debunk this misconception, it is necessary to delve into the realms of both science and mathematics. It is crucial to acknowledge that the earth orbits the sun, resulting in a consistent cycle every twenty-four hours. The mathematical calculation involves dividing one full rotation (360 degrees) by the number of hours, yielding the degrees per hour ($360 \div 24 = 15$). The discrepancy arises when we examine various scientifically accepted techniques that utilize the outstretched hand to measure angles, indicating that the entire fist (thumb and fingers) is roughly equivalent to 10 degrees. Consequently, there is a minimum difference of five degrees. Assuming the entire hand represents 10 degrees, each finger would account for 10 minutes, totaling 40 minutes.

The angle of the sun varies depending on the viewer's location in terms of longitude and latitude, as well as the time of year. These variations can have a slight impact on mathematical calculations.

This method is considered a fallacy rather than a myth due to its complete accuracy at a specific latitude, namely 57°

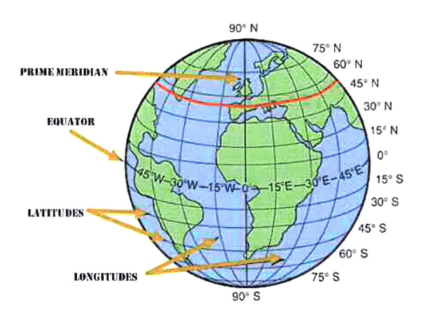

Lie: the sun is yellow.

The sun is white rather than yellow. It appears yellow to us because the Earth's atmosphere scatters blue light more efficiently than red light, leading our eyes to interpret the light as yellow. The sun emits a mixture of all colors, which we perceive as white.

Fallacy: most of the earth's oxygen is produced by trees.

Trees and rainforests contribute approximately 28 percent of the world's oxygen supply. However, the oceans play a more significant role, generating between 50 to 70 percent of oxygen, primarily through phytoplankton. An average human inhales about 550 liters of oxygen daily, while a single mature oak tree can produce nearly 275 liters each day. Phytoplankton, which are tiny organisms residing on the water's surface, harness sunlight to create energy via photosynthesis. Like terrestrial plants and trees, they absorb carbon dioxide and release oxygen. Due to their minuscule size, thousands of phytoplankton can exist in just one drop of water.

Fallacy: there are five senses.

It is commonly accepted that humans possess five primary senses: sight, smell, touch, hearing, and taste. However, some research suggests that there could be as many as 33 distinct senses, with a consensus among many scientists that at least nine senses are recognized today. In addition to the traditional five senses, the additional four that contribute to this total of nine include proprioception, thermoception, equilibrioception, and interoception.

Proprioception, also known as kinesthesia, refers to the body's capacity to perceive its own movement, actions, and position in space. This sense is distributed throughout all muscles, enabling the body to execute movements instinctively, without the need for conscious thought regarding each step taken.

Thermoception pertains to the ability to perceive temperature, specifically distinguishing between hot and cold sensations. This sensory experience is facilitated by specialized channels in the skin that react to temperature fluctuations, which can be affected by various factors, including inflammation. This sense is crucial for detecting extreme heat, prompting the body to reflexively withdraw a hand as a protective response. Ongoing research continues to explore the mechanisms behind this sensory function.

Equilibrioception, or the sense of balance, involves the perception of balance and spatial orientation. This sense plays a vital role in helping the body maintain stability and prevent falls while standing or moving. It operates in conjunction with other factors, such as perception and cognitive processes, to ensure effective balance.

Interoception refers to the sensory system that conveys information about the internal conditions of the body. This system plays a crucial role in maintaining bodily regulation and facilitating various functions. It includes sensations that indicate when one is hungry, needs to use the restroom, or requires breathing. Understanding interoception is thought to be vital for managing mental health issues, including anxiety, depression, and panic attacks. When discussions arise about internal rhythms, such as those related to sleep, hunger, or time, they are essentially addressing this sensory awareness.

APPENDIXES

Survivability Factors

Factors that affect how long a person can survive without food/water:

- Age
- Body Composition
- Environment
- Gender
- Health
- Height
- Medications
- Physical Activities
- Starting weight
- Water intact affects food needs.

Starvation timeline (generalized):

- After one day: bodies sugar reserves are depleted. Sugar (glucose) is the body's main source of energy.
- Two – Three days: fatty tissues are broken down. Fatty-tissues are used to form ketones another form energy in the body. Muscles start to use fatty tissue as it is the main source of energy.
- One week: body switches to using protein as the fatty tissues are gone. Most people's muscles will start to break down to obtain protein. More fatty tissue a person has the longer this process is delayed. People with little fatty tissue will start in less than a week.
- 14 days: muscle breakdown increases. Liver, kidney, and heart function diminish.

Exposure factors:

- Age
- Body composition
- Clothing
- Environmental controls (i.e., heating/air units, fire, etc.).
- Food/water intake
- Gender
- Health
- Height
- Mental fortitude
- Physical activities
- Physical conditioning
- Shelter
- Temperature
- Weather
- Nutrition

Environmental factors that affect survival:

- Temperature
- Wind chill
- Humidity
- Pollutants
- Weather.
- Sunlight

How to Make Lye

Lye or Sodium Hydroxide (NaOH) is an odorless, white, or slightly yellow, flakey, or lumpy material. Typically used to make soap or a component in alkaline batteries. Also called Caustic soda. Potassium Hydroxide or Caustic Potash (KOH) that look the same way is used to make liquid soap. Both Sodium Hydroxide and Potassium Hydroxide are called lye.

Prepper is mainly concerned with the Sodium Hydroxide Lye as it uses wood ash to create. Wood ash contains ten times the amount of potassium as sodium. Either version is acceptable for biodiesel, but preppers are more likely to use Sodium Hydroxide because of the ease of acquiring wood.

CAUTION: lye is listed as a hazardous material. Care should be taken not to inhale the material at any time of the making process. Lye is corrosive to the skin so long sleeves and gloves are recommended when handling. Safety glasses are used to prevent blindness. Lye is also corrosive to metals such as tin and aluminum. Contact with metal can result in hydrogen, a combustible gas.

Antiquated uses for lye:

- Laundry and Washing
- Dressing Leather
- Curing certain foods
- Preserving some products
- Rinsing hair before shampooing (fluffs & softens).
- Soap making.

Components required:
- Water
- Ash

Soft water is required. Do not use tape water because of the added minerals and/or chemicals in the water. Rainwater is the cheapest version available. Distilled water is used.

Ash made from hard wood is preferred as hard wood contains more potassium than soft wood. Optimal woods are Beech, ash, hickory, apple, cherry, birch, elm, oak, walnut, & maple. Wood needs to be burned to ash and cooled.

There are three basic home brewed methods of making lye at home. This appendix only talks about the ash barrel method because the appendix is to give a general idea of the process to show the reader why the pertinent section in the book would be considered a myth, lie, or fallacy.

Three lye making methods:

1. Ash bucket method
2. Barrel method
3. Cooking method

Barrell Method

- Take a one-gallon plastic bucket (traditionally a wooden bucket or Barrell was used)
    - Clay pots where also used at one point.
- Place a hole in bucket one inch from the bottom and plug with cork.
    - Commercial plastic spigots can be bought to attach to the bucket as an alternative.
    - A large iron or steel nail can also be used to make a hole. Leave the nails in place.
- Elevate the bucket a few inches over the ground and place a drain bucket under the cork hole in case of leaking. DO NOT use metal containers.
- Fill the bottom of bucket with one layer of rock. Alternatively, twigs can be used.
- Place a thin layer of hay on top of the rocks.
- Fill bucket with wood ash. Patting down the ash to compress the ash.
- Fill the ash bucket with soft water slowly until ash is completely saturated.
- Let the water sit for several hours (most leave overnight).

- Remove the plug or open the spigot to drain the water into the other container.
- The result is lye water.

Testing Method:

An antique way to test if the water is correct that sounds like a myth but is true is to use an egg. If the egg sinks, then it is not correct. If it mostly floats to the surface. A potato can also be used. The proper pH should be 13 if using a measuring device.

How to Make Vegetable Oil

Vegetable oil is a type of oil derived from plants. Vegetable oil can be created using a wide variety of ingredients such as seeds, nuts, fruits, and vegetables. Prepper may be familiar with the need of creating oil for its use in soaps, lotions, and cooking. Within the context of this book vegetable oil was mentioned to demonstrate the complexity of creating biodiesel. Out of all components needed for biodiesel, vegetable oil is probably the easiest to make.

Survival uses:

- Fire accelerant
- Rust Proofing
- Lighting
- Lubrication
- Cooking.
- Healing (coconut oil).
- Nose bleeds (coconut oil). *Not proven*
- Chapped lips (vegetable oil)
- Sunburns & skin care Soothing effect
- Bug bites. Remove irritation
- Athletes foot (tea tree oil). *Debatable but more on the correct side.*
- Preservation of food. *Temporarily when submerged in oil.*

List below is what preppers/survivalist use the most to make oil from:

- Sunflower seeds
- Pumpkin seeds
- Sesame seeds
- Coconut
- Avocados
- Walnuts
- Hazelnuts
- Peanuts

Yields:

Sunflower	5.3 pounds
Pumpkin	5.3 pounds
Walnuts	2.9 pounds
Hazelnuts	3.6 pounds
Peanuts	4.6 pounds

Making:

The most used prepper method of making vegetable oil is to use sunflower seeds. Sunflowers are inexpensive and easy to grow. There are two types of sunflower seeds; confectionary (the ones we eat) and black oil (bird seed). Black oil is supposed to produce twice the oil as confectionary. The simplest way is to use a vegetable press. Ensure seeds and nuts are de-hulled.

- Set up the machine
- Fill the heating unit with the recommended flammable and light it.
- Allow it to heat (approximately 10 min)
- Pour seeds into the hopper
- Crank the machine for about 20 minutes. Should get about 14 ounces of oil.
- Remove your container of fresh oil and cap tightly
- Oil should be black if using black seed. After setting for a few days sediment will settle at the bottom.
- Siphon off the oil and discard the sediment
- Oil can be stored for up to two years in a tightly sealed container and cool, dry place.

Closing:

Coconut, avocado, plants fibers, and animal fats all have very different methods to create oil. The ease of obtainability, versatility, and creation vary with each type. The left-over product called seed pulp can be fed to chickens as a protein additive or used as compost in gardening.

A trick that works to reuse cooking oil is to drop potato skins into the used oil and allow them to soak it up. Remove the skin and strain the oil through a cheesecloth. The oil continues to get darker with each use. Remember it will eventually go bad so get it separated from unused oil and taste test before use. Used cooking oil can be safely used in biodiesel creation but adds steps to the process.

Raw Food List

The following list is not all inclusive and includes easily obtained products found in a grocery store. See the next page for a list of wild plants that can be consumed raw.

Fruits	Vegetables	Nuts/Seeds	Grains	Legumes	Other
Apples	Asparagus	Cashews	Wheat	Black Beans	Honey[1]
Bananas	Eggplant	Almonds	Rice	Kidney Beans	Agave Nectar[1]
Pears	Spinach	Hazelnuts	Buckwheat	White Beans	Maple Syrup*
Apricots	Kale	Brazil Nuts	Quinoa	Navy Beans	Milk[1]
Peaches	Broccoli	Pecans	Oats	Butter Beans	Cheese[1]
Plums	Squash	Walnuts	Amaranth	Lentils	Yogurt[1]
Avocados	Zucchini	Pine Nuts	Spelt	Chickpeas	Palm Oil*
Blackberries	Sweet Potatoes	Sunflower Seeds	Rye	Red Peans	Coconut Oil*
Strawberries	Potatoes	Sesame Seeds	Barley	Peanuts	Palm Oil*
Blueberries	Artichokes	Pumpkin Seeds	Teff		
Raspberries	Cucumbers	Hemp Seeds			
Cherries	Lettuce	Flax Seeds			
Mangos	Onions	Chia Seeds			
Papayas	Garlic				
Lemons	Peppers				
Oranges	Cauliflower				
Grapefruit	Fiddleheads				
Limes	Peas				
Coconut	Green Beans				
Grapes	Wax Beans				
Tomatoes	Corn				

* = Unprocessed   1 = Raw

It's important to note that while a lot of food can be eaten in its raw state not all foods can be tolerated raw by everyone. Some of its commonly eaten raw also have additives to make the food more tolerable. Seeds and nuts for example are most consumed when salted. Grains can be consumed raw but are hard to tolerate when not cooked and when they are consumed raw, they are almost always mixed with other things.

Below is not a complete list of wild plants that are considered safe for human consumption. Safety does not mean enjoyable or tolerable. Most of the plants will not be enjoyed but will sustain a life. Not all the parts are edible on all plants. Lists include commonly consumed plants, fruits, berries, and mushrooms.

Common Name	Scientific Name	Regions	Parts
Amaranth	Amaranthus Retroflexus	Asia, Africa, Caribbean	Whole Plant
Asparagus	Aspargus Officinalis	N. Americas	
Bamboo	Bambusoidae	Asia, Americas	Shoots
Bluebead	Clintonia Borealis	Americas	Leaves (other parts poisonous)
Broadleaf Plantain	Plantago Major	Eurasia	Leaves
Bardock	Arctium Lappa	Europe.	Leaves, Flower stalk, roots
Catnip	Nepeta Cataria	Europe. N. America	Leaves, young flower,
Cattail	Typha	N. America	Roots, Flower spikes, Pollen, Inner plant parts
Chickweed	Sterllaria Media	Europe	Leaves
Chicory	Cichorium Intybus	Europe. N. America	
Clovers	Trifolium	Americas	All Parts
Coltsfoot	Tussilago farfara	N. America	Flower, Stems, Leaves
Coneflower	Echinacea Purporea	N. America	Leaves, Petals
Curied Dock	Rumex Crispus	N. America	Leaves
Dandelion	Taraxacum Officinale	Eurasia, Americas	Whole Plants
Fiddleheads	Matteuccia Struthioptens	N. America	Fern Part
Fireweed	Epilobium Angustifolium	Americas	Flower, Leaves
Garlic Mustard	Alliaria Petiolate	Asia, Europe, N. America	Whole Plant
Jerusalem Artichoke	Helianthus tuberosus	America's	Tuberous root
Kelp	Laminariales spp.	Pacific Ocean	Whole Plant
Lamb Quarters	Chenopodium Album	America's	Whole plant
Milkweed	Asclepias Synaca	America's	Leaves, Flower buds, Pods
Miner's Lettuce	Claytonia Perfoliate	N. America	Flower, Leaves, Roots
Mullein	Verbascum Thapsus	Europe, Africa, Asia	Flowers, Leaves
Pickleweed	Salicornia Europeae	America's	Stem
Plantain	Plantago	Southeast Asia	
Prickly Pear Cactus	Opuntia	America	Fruit, Plant Flesh
Purslane	Portulaca Oleracea	N. Africa, Middle East, India	Flowers, Leaves, Stems
Queen Anne's Lace	Daucus Carota	Middle East, Europe, N. America	Leaves, Roots
Rose	Rosa spp	Asia, Europe, N.	Petals, Buds, Young

		America, Africa	shoots, Leaves
Self-heal	Prunella Vulgaris	Eurasia, N. America	Leaves
Sheep Sorrel	Rumex Acetosella	Eurasia	Leaves, Seeds
Stinging Nettle	Urtica Dioica	Europe, Asia, Africa	Leave, Stems, Roots
Sweet Gale	Myrica Gale	Europe, N. America	Make tea from fruit/leaves
Watercress	Nasturtium Officinale	N. America	Leaves, Stems, Flowers
White Mustard	Synapsis Alba	Africa, Europe, Middle East	
Wild Ginger	Asarum caudatan	N. America	Leaves

Identification of the plant is crucial. Many plants can look similar. Plants that look like safe plants are not always safe. Eight features of poisonous plants to know.

1. Milky or discolored sap
2. Spines, fine hairs, or thorns
3. Beans, bulbs, or seeds inside pods
4. Bitter or soapy taste
5. Dill, carrot, parsnip, umbrella or parsley-like foliage
6. "almond" scent in the woody parts & leaves
7. Grain heads in pink, purplish, or black spurs
8. Three-leaved growth pattern.

The above is long but not complete demonstrating a lot learning when it comes to foraging for edible plants. The simplest method is to recognize a few key plants common to one's area (about five). Once you get a few down like an expert then add a few more each time.

Below are the most mentioned items in survival outside normal foods:

1. Pine (Pinus spp). Specifically, pine needles are mentioned for making tea rich in vitamin C. Heat the pinecones to get seeds to eat raw.
2. Cattails (Typha latifolia or Typha angustifolia). Shoots can be eaten raw. Before the head emerges, it can be cooked and eaten like a corn cob. The pollen can be used for soup or made into flour.
3. Dandelion: flower, stem, and root can be eaten raw.
4. Most grasses: seeds can be eaten raw, added to stew, or ground into flour.
5. Prickly Pear Cactus. Pulp can be roasted. Fruit can be juiced or eaten raw.

Deaths by Natural Disasters

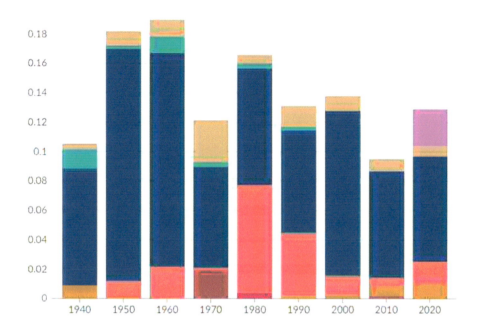

- 🟪 Droughts
- 🟧 Floods
- 🟩 Earthquakes
- 🟦 Storms
- 🟥 Extreme temperatures
- 🟥 Volcanoes
- 🟧 Wildfires
- 🟧 Glacial lake outbursts
- 🟩 Mass movements (dry)
- 🟥 Mass movements (wet)
- 🟦 Fogs

Deaths by Animals

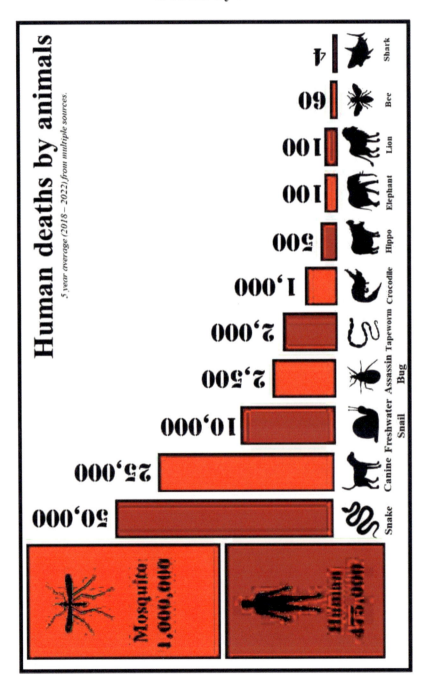

Traps

It is not possible to create universal traps that will effectively capture all animal species. It is essential to identify the specific species present in a particular area and tailor your traps accordingly.

To effectively catch animals, it is essential to position your traps and snares in locations where there is clear evidence of animal movement. Even the most well-constructed snare will be ineffective if it is randomly placed in the forest. Animals typically have designated bedding sites, water sources, and feeding grounds, all connected by trails. Therefore, it is crucial to strategically place your snares and traps in proximity to these key areas. Consider the following factors:

- Tracks
- Animal Scat or Droppings
- Animal Trails or Runs
- Nesting or Roosting Sites
- Feeding area or watering holes
- Chewed or rubbed vegetation.

Traps or snares set along a trail or pathway should incorporate channel techniques. To create an effective channel, construct a funnel-shaped barrier that extends from the edges of the trail towards the trap, ensuring that the narrowest section is closest to the trap itself. It is essential that the channel remains discreet to prevent alerting the animal. As the animal approaches the trap, it will be unable to turn left or right, compelling it to move directly into the trap. Most wild animals tend to avoid backing up, opting instead to continue in the direction they are facing. The channel does not need to be an impenetrable barrier; it simply needs to make it inconvenient for the animal to navigate over or around it. For optimal results, the channelization should narrow the trail to a width that is just slightly greater than the width of the intended target animal

To ensure successful trapping, it is essential to eliminate or conceal any human scent on and around the trap. While birds may not possess a strong sense of smell, most mammals rely heavily on their olfactory senses, often more than their vision. Even a faint trace of human scent on a trap can deter prey and lead them to avoid the vicinity. Completely removing the scent from a trap can be challenging, but masking it is relatively straightforward. Utilizing mud, especially from areas rich in decaying vegetation, can be effective. Apply it to your hands while handling the trap and to the trap itself during the setup. Additionally, animals across the globe are familiar with the odor of burned vegetation and smoke, becoming alarmed only when a fire is actively burning. Thus, smoking the components of the trap serves as an efficient method to disguise your scent.

Many animals have a natural tendency to steer clear of pitfall traps. It is advisable to assemble the different components of a trap or snare away from the intended location, transport them to the site, and then set them up. This approach minimizes disruption to the surrounding vegetation, which could otherwise signal danger to the prey. Avoid using freshly cut, live plants for constructing a trap or snare, as the sap released from these plants emits an odor that can alert the animals, serving as a warning signal.

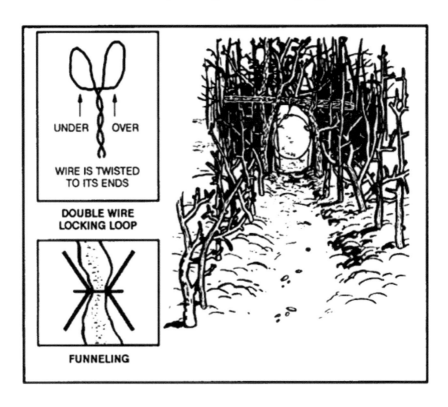

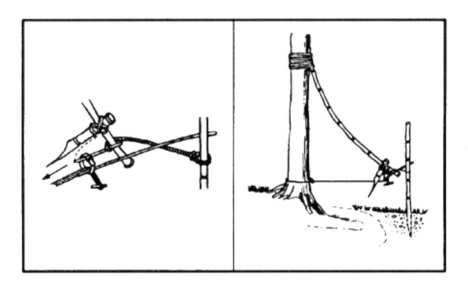

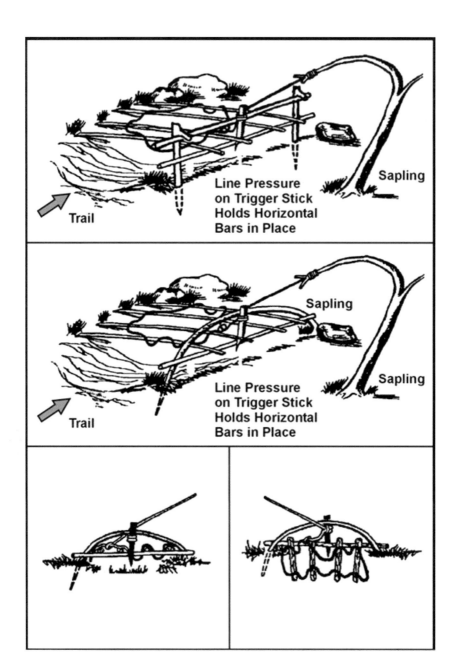

Sapling

Line Pressure
on Trigger Stick
Holds Horizontal
Bars in Place

Trail

Sapling

Sapling

Line Pressure
on Trigger Stick
Holds Horizontal
Bars in Place

Trail

Author Biography

Joshua Bromley completed his high school education in 2000 in a small rural town in Arkansas, shortly thereafter enlisting in the United States Navy within a week of his graduation. Following two weeks of boot camp, he was assigned to submarines with the intention of pursuing a career as an electrician, following in his father's footsteps. However, after the events of September 11, his focus shifted, and he became a Hospital Corpsman, providing emergency services in a hospital and primarily supporting Green Side Units alongside the United States Marine Corps. This role led him to participate in four combat deployments in Iraq and Afghanistan. Josh specialized in field and combat medicine, achieving instructor certifications as an Emergency Medical Technician, Tactical Combat Casualty Care Instructor, and Master Training Specialist, in addition to other tactical qualifications such as Firearms Instructor, Close Quarters Combat, and Foreign Military Advisor. He has received numerous honors, including the Submarine Warfare Pin, Fleet Marine Forces Warfare Pin, and Seabee Combat Warfare Pin, along with various personal and unit commendations. Additionally, he earned a Bachelor of Arts degree in Psychology during his Navy career.

At present, he serves as a Police Officer, upholding his commitment to serving the community. His main areas of focus include patrol operations and investigative work. Furthermore, he has played a vital role as a Field Training Officer and Close Combat Battle Instructor, and he continues to prioritize Tactical Medicine, albeit in an alternative setting.

Josh's personal interests encompass survivalism, psychology, medicine, and self-defense. He also has a keen interest in reading, writing, video games, and films. Additionally, he possesses proficiency in Krav Maga, Jiu-Jitsu, small arms marksmanship, and various other self-defense techniques.

Made in the USA
Columbia, SC
03 January 2025

800302bc-aa79-448e-a084-bdd7aeaf255aR01